the gaia book of

organic gardening

Foreword by
Patrick Holden
Director of the Soil Association

Gaia Books

A GAIA ORIGINAL

Books from Gaia celebrate the vision of Gaia, the
self-sustaining living Earth, and seek to help its readers
live in greater personal and planetary harmony.

Additional text	Cindy Engel
Design	Bridget Morley
Editor	Cindy Engel
Photography	Steve Teague
Production	Aileen O'Reilly
Direction	Patrick Nugent, Jo Godfrey Wood

This is a Registered Trade Mark of Gaia Books.

Distributed in the United States and Canada by
Sterling Publishing Co., Inc.
387 Park Avenue South,
New York, NY 10016–8810

ISBN 1-85675-218-6
EAN 9 781856 7521183

A catalogue record of this book is available from the British Library.

Printed and bound in China

foreword

Soil is the basis of life on earth and the survival of our planet depends on it.

Up until the advent of artificial fertilizers and pesticides, farmers and gardeners had to look after their soil in order to produce good healthy crops. The industrialization of agriculture, after the First World War, changed this. In 1946, a group of organic pioneers saw the vital role that soil plays in health and formed The Soil Association to protect our soils against the threat they perceived. In the decades that followed, as predicted, soil erosion increased, and the mineral levels in fruit and vegetables declined. Government figures show that between 1940 and 1991, levels of some minerals fell by 76 per cent.

In contrast, growing evidence shows that organic fruit and vegetables generally contain more nutrients than non-organic food. While awaiting further scientific evidence on the benefits of organic crops compared to non-organic, trust your intuition. Compare a freshly grown local and organic carrot with a non-organic one grown with chemicals. I believe you will notice the difference.

Organic growers protect the soil by harnessing natural processes and consequently produce healthy crops full of vitality. This book will increase your understanding of how a healthy soil is crucial to our health and the health of the planet.

Patrick Holden
Director
The Soil Association

contents

work with nature rather than against it

Organic gardening is more than gardening without artificial chemicals. And it is certainly more than doing nothing to your garden. It is gardening with nature rather than against it; a system that imitates and enhances the natural cycle of fertility.

It isn't simply a matter of swapping artificial sprays for natural ones, but an integrated approach by which you help your garden to help you by observing and learning about the processes at work in your garden, and recognising how best to work with them.

In the past, gardeners produced bountiful food and beautiful ornamentals through hands-on husbandry. They nurtured the soil, recycled waste, made what they needed from biodegradable local sources, saved their own seeds, outwitted weeds, pests, and disease, and carefully planned what to plant, when and where. They didn't call themselves organic gardeners. They just practised good gardening. With the rise of the petrochemical industry in the middle of the last century came the advent of the quick fix for seemingly every farming

Why organic gardening is good for you

❀ No risk of accidental poisoning from toxic chemicals used in the garden.

❀ No risk of toxic pesticide residues or artificial preservatives in food.

❀ Vitamins break down easily during storage, so fresh food from your garden provides a vitamin-packed diet.

❀ Organic vegetables grown in well-nourished soil contain a range of minerals and trace elements that are often missing or found in only low concentrations in chemically reared crops.

❀ Organic fruits and vegetables are rich in their own protective phytochemicals (see page 11). Scientists are finding that many of these are protective against cancer and other diseases.

❀ The physical exercise, fresh air, and sunlight of hands-on gardening is good for you.

❀ If you include chickens and small livestock in your organic garden, you will also provide yourself with meat and eggs free from hormones, antibiotics, and potentially harmful drug residues.

Why your organic garden is good for all of us

❀ No dangerous chemicals leak into the surrounding environment.

❀ Sustainable management of resources helps us all.

❀ Recycling and reusing materials reduces the use of finite landfill sites.

❀ The soil is improved for future generations rather than degraded and impoverished.

❀ Biodiversity is maximised, so providing a rich source of genetic variety for present and future generations to draw upon.

❀ Sourcing materials locally helps us all by reducing transport pollution and congestion.

and gardening problem: inorganic sprays to kill pests, weeds, and disease, and artificial fertilisers to boost growth and productivity. The temptation of more for less was understandably enticing.

But the trouble with quick fixes is that they inevitably lead to other problems in the longer run. This has certainly been the case with chemical warfare gardening. Insecticides such as organo-phosphates were developed as nerve gas agents and have to be handled with great care. Synthetic pesticides and fertilisers knock out nature's natural cycles, checks and balances, harm wildlife, and contaminate our food and water.

Scientists blame pesticides for a range of health problems including cancer and immune and reproductive dysfunction in both animals and humans. Few of the early gardening chemicals are still in legal use. Each year more are taken off the market as evidence of health dangers emerges.

WORKING WITH NATURE

There are pests to deal with in the garden, but don't rush to exterminate too much life. There's a reason why it's there. Biological controls have always existed to keep pests down, as pests are also food sources for creatures that may pollinate your flowers, eat debris, keep other pests off your plants, keep the soil in good condition, or a thousand and one other helpful functions.

Pesticides can make a pest situation worse. If you keep applying pesticides, the intended pests will eventually adapt or become resistant to the chemicals you are throwing at them. Or secondary pests that are not affected by the chemicals will become primary pests. So more and different chemicals have to be developed to get rid of the secondary pest, adding to the existing cocktail of chemicals that is being released into your garden, harming plants and soil as well as pests. Blanket application of pesticides doesn't stop at killing pests – it also kills life that you need in your garden.

MAKE PEACE NOT WAR

'If it moves, kill it' has been too popular for too long. Gardeners who follow this school of thought may end up with a shiny, tidy garden, but the only way they'll keep that up is through ever-increasing arrays of toxic chemicals. Once you start using artificial ways of maintaining your garden, it's far too easy to become reliant on them and create a vicious circle. Using chemical pesticides may seem a simple way of

Agricultural (and horticultural) pesticides are made from petrochemicals, based on oil, a non-renewable resource. Modern agricultural processes are very oil-energy intensive in the fuel they use directly to power machinery and indirectly to make fertilisers and pesticides. This is estimated at 2.6% of total energy usage in the UK.

43% of all non-organic fruit and vegetables contain detectable levels of pesticide residues.

Pesticides such as the organophosphate nerve poisons have infiltrated every corner of our world and made their way into our food chain. In a recent survey of school children in the US, 92% had metabolites of organophosphates in their urine.

At least 150 pesticides are potential human carcinogens (cause cancer).

Agricultural biodiversity is shrinking as fewer species and varieties are made available for cultivation. Today 75% of global food supply comes from a mere twelve crop species. Not only are we losing species diversity but we are also losing varieties within those species.

Modern processing replaces herbs rich in phytochemicals with artificial chemical preservatives, taste-enhancers, and colourants. Our industrial diet is greatly weakened thereby in both nutritional and medicinal attributes.

Phytochemicals

Plants contain many chemicals that are bioactive – that is, they affect living organisms such as ourselves. Many are medicinal and have been proven protective against diseases such as cancer and even the effects of ageing.

There are hundreds of beneficial phytochemicals (plant chemicals) already identified, but many more still to be investigated. The greater the diversity of plants in our diet, the greater the range of beneficial phytochemicals we consume.

Plant foods with the highest anti-cancer activity include garlic, soybean, ginger, liquorice root, broccoli, and cabbage.

Throw away sprays and start to think organic. Learn how good garden practices and specific planting can encourage natural biological controls. Find ways of limiting disease and pests, so they don't become a problem.

killing or controlling pests, but pesticides do not solve the complex problem of maintaining a healthy balance in your garden. They are like any drug: they artificially prop up a system for a short while, but in the longer term they will destroy your garden's health.

Your soil contains thousands of organisms working together to keep it healthy and fertile. Worms and insects drag rotting material down into the soil, digest and excrete it and transform it into plant food, with the help of soil bacteria, fungi, and algae. When inorganic herbicides get into your soil they kill off these important organisms that are responsible for keeping your soil healthy and releasing plant nutrients. This means that nutrients in the soil are not made available and plants can't get at them, so your plants become weaker until they can't support themselves. Gardeners then become ever more reliant on artificial inputs – chemical fertilisers, herbicides, and more pesticides – just to keep things going.

There is another way. Some say it is too much hard work: weeding, looking out for pests and diseases, planning, composting, and the rest. But with good management and efficient planning, organic gardening is a pleasure not a hardship.

How do I garden without artificial chemicals?

The short answer is vigilance. By keeping an eye on your garden you will notice pests and disease before they escalate to problem levels. Organic sprays are available, but they should be used only as a last resort. The most effective agent of control in any organic garden is always you, the gardener.

There is no mystery to gardening. There are no such people as green-fingered gardeners. But like everything else there are certain basic rules that are simple once you understand how they work, puzzling if you don't. The best gardens are not created in an instant; they develop gradually. Organic gardeners work with nature, so you should learn to think about what your garden wants from you as well as what you want from it.

There is no substitute for building and maintaining a healthy soil, for considered planting and constant vigilance. The most important organic pest and disease control is simply good gardening practice. Being an organic gardener is not about going back in time, but rather about going forward into a sustainable form of modern gardening, using the latest understanding of the fertility cycle, so that we can make the most of what nature can do for us.

Good organic practice

Get organised

With good planning you will minimise effort and maximise rewards. Knowing when to look for weeds, pests, and disease, when to feed, and when to leave your plants alone, are all important aspects of successful organic gardening.

Feed and support the soil rather than the plants

A well-structured soil that is full of organic matter will support strong plants. Pest and disease first attack weaker plants. Fertile soil will also provide plenty of food for many flying, crawling and burrowing creatures so they will be less instantly attracted to your cultivated plants. If your soil is enriched with garden compost, this provides an additional measure of protection as nutrient-enriched soil suppresses soil-borne pests and diseases.

Cover ground

Reduce the amount of bare ground at all times by mulching, growing cover crops or planting close together to reduce opportunities for weeds.

Match plants to your garden

Good planning is essential. If, for example, you try to grow Mediterranean plants in a cold, wet soil, or lime-loving plants in an acid soil, you'll never have much success. The plants will be weak and susceptible to every pest and disease that's doing the rounds. For best results plant plants that are adapted to the particular conditions you have in particular locations within the garden.

Intercrop

Interplanting a mixture of different crops provides structural support, shade, and protection against wind.

Maximise biodiversity

A natural ecosystem is not a monoculture. If you concentrate on one or two species you are asking for problems as pests and disease will have no difficulty getting stuck in. But if you grow a good mixture of plants they will attract a wide range of insects and other organisms so the predator–pest ratio should be reasonably balanced and nature's system of checks and balances will be able to operate.

Rotate

Avoid growing the same food crop in the same place year on year to reduce the chance of pests and disease building up. Similarly, with ornamentals, should disease knock out one species, plant something completely different in its place.

Distinguish friend from foe

Learn which creatures are your allies against pests and encourage them into the garden by providing the plants and conditions they prefer. Provide them with friendly habitats, including sources of water and hiding places, if necessary.

Get physical

Devise barriers and traps to keep pests out, and prevent spread of disease or weeds. These can be simple measures such as netting trees and soft fruit to prevent bird damage, covering crops with horticultural fleece to keep flying insects off, or digging in deep barriers to prevent weed roots spreading. A well-timed physical removal of weeds can prevent the need for herbicides later.

Practise safe gardening

Keep an eye out for disease; remove and burn all diseased material as soon as you find it. At the end of the growing season in the autumn, clear the ground. Don't bring diseased plants into your garden. Similarly, don't bring toxic or potentially dangerous materials into your garden in the form of chemically treated wood or genetically modified seeds.

Recycle and reuse

Keep the cycle of fertility as closed as possible. Return non-toxic biodegradable materials to the soil via the compost heap. Recycle your domestic waste. Save your own seeds. Find ways to reuse materials so that the environment is not harmed by the production of unnecessary new products. In other words, aim to make your garden sustainable – not reliant on finite resources or on producing harmful pollution.

Introduce biological controls

Use acceptable organic sprays as a last resort. If you can't get pest attack under control with cultivation, traps or barriers, other options are possible as a last resort. Microbial pesticides are made from bacteria that occur naturally in the soil. Or there are pesticides made from petals, seeds, and roots, or sprays from soaps and natural oils.

Be tolerant

Accept that nature is not a sterile environment. Decide which pests and weeds you can tolerate, and those you can't. Something that seems reasonable to one gardener might drive another one crazy. I've learnt to live with a level of slug destruction, but flea beetles drive me to distraction. Concentrate on what bothers you most. Similarly, decide how much yield reduction you can tolerate. A few blemishes may be an acceptable price to pay for organic produce.

Creating balance

Over the years, you and your garden will find a dynamic balance where pests, disease, and difficulties are minimised while growth, productivity, and beauty are maximised. You will reap a harvest of food and ornamentals without harming yourself or others, and at the same time create a sanctuary of biodiversity bringing lifelong enjoyment.

Decay

At the end of the growing season or life of the plant, it rots down, returning nutrients to the soil.

Dung and death

Animal excrement adds to soil fertility. Eventually their carcasses, too, rot down, adding essential nutrients back to the soil.

Fruits and seeds

If pollination is successful seeds develop. Some plants produce attractive edible fruits around their seeds to encourage animals to eat them and spread the seeds far and wide.

Some plants store foods in specialised organs, such as potato tubers, to live off during the leaner part of the year. Animals like to eat these, too.

THE NATURAL CYCLE OF FERTILITY

Dormancy

Ripe seeds are distributed or fall to the ground, where they wait for the right conditions to germinate.

Germination

Those seeds that germinate successfully have to compete with other plants for food, space, and sunlight.

They also have to fight off pests and disease.

Flowers and pollination

Flowering is a call for pollination.

Insects can be essential pollinators for many garden plants.

Growth

Plant growth requires nutrients from the soil and water, as well as adequate warmth, air, and sunlight.

soil

*civilisations which have neglected
their soil have perished*

soil

You can't grow healthy plants in undernourished soil, but once you get your soil right you'll have no problems growing what you want, where you want it.

Start with the soil

If you buy a plant from a nursery, dig a hole in unprepared soil and put it straight in – it may grow. It probably will survive for one season, but then it will run into problems. You could simply blame the plant, or the supplier, and try again, perhaps feeding the plant at some stage. You will probably have limited success. If you put another similar plant into a bed of well-nourished soil, it will flourish. This isn't magic, just sound common sense. Soil is the basic building block in our gardens. If you get that right, everything else will follow.

Plants need many of the same things as humans: air, water, and food. The soil should supply these needs, providing nutrition in forms that plants can use. Plants feed through their roots, which need to be able to delve and spread through the soil. If it is fertile – in good condition and full of nutrition – you'll have contented plants; if not, they'll have a hard time. People can survive for a while on junk food, but they won't be healthy. It's the same with plants: if you give them poor soil they are stressed, vulnerable to disease and pests, and unable to reach their potential.

What is soil?

There is much more to soil than immediately meets the eye. It is a heaving world of different life forms and minerals; a mixture of air, water, weathered rocks and organic matter, broken down by the actions of billions of living creatures and tiny organisms. Healthy soil is a natural chemical factory, teeming with life, where millions of micro-organisms convert minerals and chemicals into substances plants can use to grow. You need to provide the right environment for these processes to take place. It's not difficult to keep your soil healthy, and it is entirely rewarding.

Imagine how difficult it must be for all these processes to go on in a very dry, thin, hard soil, or if it is solid, wet, and airless; how much easier everything must be if the soil is deep, moist, and crumbly. If your soil is going to support plant life year after year, you must look after it, otherwise it will eventually support little or nothing at all. This is what happens to land fed year on year with artificial fertilisers – all

Soil is alive: a mineral, animal, and vegetable base, teeming with organisms that work together to keep everything in the optimum condition needed to support healthy plants.

its own natural goodness is used up and fertility comes purely through artificial additives. The soil becomes useful only to keep plants from toppling over and to provide water.

Organic gardeners feed their soil with slow-release garden compost and well-rotted manures. This ensures that all the soil creatures, from microbes to earthworms, can play their full role in producing healthy crops.

What's in my soil?

PLANT FOOD

The bulk of soil is tiny crumbs of minerals. How they are distributed depends on climate and cultivation, as well as the underlying rock formation. Plants absorb the minerals they need through their roots in solution from the water in the soil. Mixed with the mineral particles is other plant food in the form of animal wastes and the remains of dead plants and animals.

Any organic matter that falls on the soil surface will eventually be incorporated into it as weathering, living creatures and tiny organisms start the process of decomposition. Worms and insects drag rotting material down, digest and excrete it and begin transforming it into humus. Soil bacteria, fungi, and algae then release the nutrients from humus in a form plants can use. So all organic matter is transformed in the soil into more useable minerals, plus the proteins, carbohydrates, and sugars that plants and soil organisms need. Then plants grow, providing food for insects and animals, falling plant matter, and manure is deposited onto the soil again and the natural cycle of soil fertility continues.

AIR AND WATER

Plants need oxygen just as much as humans. They take it in through their roots and give out carbon dioxide. The living organisms in the soil also need oxygen to speed up the decaying processes that turn organic matter into nutrition. Oxygen enters the soil via the passages made by burrowing creatures, through the spaces between crumbs of soil and from the air brought in with water draining down through the soil.

The nearer the soil-air is to the surface, the greater its oxygen content; at lower levels soil-air contains more carbon dioxide. If soil is not sufficiently aerated it contains an unhealthy balance of carbon dioxide to oxygen, which can poison plant roots and living organisms.

Not all the living creatures in soil are helpful ones. Most soils also contain some pests and disease organisms, but once you get to know how your soil works you should be able to manage to reduce potential problems.

Photosynthesis and respiration

Green plants make the food they need, using sunlight in a process called photosynthesis. This process combines simple carbon dioxide and water molecules into complex carbohydrates. Photosynthesis takes in carbon dioxide and gives off waste oxygen.

However, plant cells also need to respire, like animals cells do. For this they need to take in oxygen and give off carbon dioxide.

Given adequate levels of oxygen, carbon dioxide and warmth, cell respiration takes place continuously, but photosynthesis requires light and so normally only occurs during the day.

Earthworms are your natural aeration system. Their tunnels allow air to permeate deep below the soil surface.

It has been calculated that a single earthworm can shift 30 tonnes of earth in its lifetime.

You can get an idea of your soil's fertility by checking out the worm population. Turn over a section of soil about 45cm in length and a spade's depth. A fertile soil that has been regularly fed with muck and compost will probably provide about 30 worms in that small area – about half would be a good start. You won't find many worms in a heavily compacted clay soil as it's too hard for them to move through and they can drown in waterlogged soil. You probably won't find many in light sandy soil either, as worms are very susceptible to drought.

The water content of soil is equally crucial. Plants get food in solution through their roots. If there isn't enough soil-water they can't absorb necessary nutrients and starve. Thirsty plants can't make efficient use of sunlight, as photosynthesis can't proceed. On the other hand, if plants get too much water they can't absorb the air they need, so they drown and rot.

Soil structure

All soil – except for peat, which is a special case – is made up of three layers of rock in different stages of decomposition, although these layers are sometimes rather indistinct.

Topsoil is dark brown and crumbly, full of organic matter and teeming with life. Most plant activity takes place here.

Below topsoil is **subsoil**. This is made up mainly of rock particles and is usually paler than topsoil because it contains little organic matter. Here there is less plant activity, although deep-rooted plants mine the subsoil for nutrients. Subsoil contains few living organisms, but much of the water that plants need is stored here, along with important minerals waiting to be made available to growing plants.

Beneath subsoil is **bedrock**, the basis of all soil.

Topsoil

Subsoil

Bedrock

Identifying my soil

The first step when you take on a garden is to identify the type of soil you'll be working with. To do this you will need to assess your soil structure, texture, drainage, acidity, and check for signs of nutrient deficiencies.

SOIL TEXTURE

When we talk about sand, clay, or loam soils we are referring to the size of the mineral particles or the soil's texture. Sandy soils have large particles, which means they don't bind together closely and there are significant spaces between the particles. They are sometimes referred to as 'light' soils and they are easy to work, but hard to keep in good condition as they tend to drain fast.

Clay soils are made up of tiny mineral particles which stick together like glue and provide a large surface area. Clay soils tend to be solid and heavy to work, and difficult for air and water to penetrate, so they can get stale or waterlogged, but they hold nutrients well. Silt soils have slightly larger particles than clay and are easier to work, but get sticky and cold when wet and dry into dust.

Loam soils are made of a mixture of small and large particles. They are usually divided into sandy loams and clay loams, depending on the proportion of clay particles they contain. Peat soils also contain a mixture of small and large particles.

IDENTITY CHECK

The easiest check is just to pick up a small handful and try to roll it into a ball in the palm of your hand. If it feels gritty and refuses to stick together, it is sand. If it is slightly gritty but forms a soft dark ball, it is loam, and a soft springy dark ball is peat. If it makes a sticky ball, it is clay or silt but if you can make the surface shine when you rub your thumb over it, you're holding clay.

ASSESSING SUBSOIL

Looking at the subsoil gives you a good idea of your soil's good points and problem areas. Blue-grey subsoil indicates lack of oxygen and therefore poor drainage. On the other hand, reddish or yellow subsoil indicates high levels of oxidation from the action of air on the weathering rocks. If air is getting through the soil it is also likely to have good drainage. However, if there appears to be a band of red or brown subsoil up to half a metre below the surface this is probably

Clay particles are much too small to see, at around 0.0002mm diameter.
Sand particles range from 0.2–2mm diameter. Anything larger is gravel.

Even an area of predominantly sandy soil may have clay or loam pockets, or vice versa, depending on the underlying geology. Soil in different areas of your garden may also behave differently, depending on the levels of cultivation.

Peat soils are in a class of their own. They are formed not from rock, but from vegetable matter which has been compressed under water and has not rotted away. Naturally drained peatlands are the most fertile soils in the world.

Assess the texture of your soil by rubbing it between your fingers.

hardpan – a layer of compacted soil. This is usually caused by the action of heavy machinery on the soil surface, or sometimes by bad drainage.

SOIL ACIDITY

If vegetable growth in your garden is poor, or soil is moss-covered with a rather stagnant look, or you have lots of weed growth, particularly sorrel and docks, you should purchase a kit to check the pH of your soil. This indicates whether your soil contains too little or too much calcium, or how acid or alkaline it is. The neutral point on the scale is pH7; soils below that become increasingly acid (too little calcium) and above pH7 are increasingly alkaline (too much).

The most fertile soil for growing vegetables is very slightly acid, from just below pH6 to just above pH7. Most trees and shrubs and herbaceous plants will also grow happily in soil with this pH, but some fruits prefer slightly more acid conditions.

If the calcium content is off-balance, this can affect the availability of other elements in the soil – in very acid or very alkaline soils plant roots have difficulty in extracting whatever minerals may be available to them. It can also harm or deter the soil organisms that keep your soil healthy, so it is important to get it right.

In some gardens there may be pockets within quite a small area which are considerably more acid or alkaline, depending on the underlying geology as well as how much the soil has been worked, so regular testing is an excellent way of getting to know your soil.

In **very alkaline** soils, plants may be unable to get at the micronutrients they need. Iron, copper, and manganese, for example, become locked up in insoluble compounds.

Hardpan is very common in gardens on new housing developments. Whereas you should generally leave subsoil well alone and concentrate on cultivating the topsoil, you will need to break up any hardpan as it forms an impervious layer preventing good drainage and nutrients getting to the plant.

ACID SOILS

Soils in cooler damp climates, such as the UK, tend to become increasingly acid, even if well cultivated, as rain is constantly washing calcium out of the soil. If your soil is very acid, aim to bring the pH up slowly, over three or more seasons. The usual way to correct an acid soil is to add ground lime to it. Lime also improves the structure of clay soils by helping the particles to stick together in crumbs, and it inhibits bacteria that remove nitrogen from the soil. But it's not the only solution. One problem with lime is that earthworms don't like it, so it may take a while for soil life to build up again after liming.

Over-liming causes its own problems, inhibiting plant growth by suppressing the actions of some important trace elements. On sandy soil, dress the surface with around 200 grams of lime per square metre; loamy soil will take more, and heavy clay more still.

Wait several months before applying muck to an area you have limed, as the reaction between lime and manure will cause the escape of ammonia as a gas, wasting nitrogen that could otherwise be used by the soil. Apply ground limestone to the surface of the soil in autumn, before cultivating in spring.

ALKALINE SOILS

It is rare for cultivated soils to be over-alkaline, as regular applications of muck and compost will usually supply all the elements soil needs, apart from lime. Most vegetables will grow in slightly alkaline soil. If you can't lower your soil's alkaline level with regular cultivation, you can apply gypsum or powdered sulphur at the rate of 130 grams per square metre. You will be more likely to succeed in creating fertile growing conditions if you build raised beds (see page 95) or dig some trenches and fill them with imported acid soil to get plants going.

Do not lime an area of the garden where you intend to grow tomatoes or potatoes the following season, as they are sensitive to excessive lime. Brassicas, on the other hand, love recently limed soil.

pH scale

pH4–5 Acid.
Found in cold, wet areas.
Camellias and rhododendrons thrive, also blueberries and cranberries.
Few earthworms; little soil life.

pH5–6 Fairly acid.
Typical of unimproved soil in very wet areas.
Potatoes, tomatoes, and most fruits thrive.

pH6–7 Neutral.
Most plants and garden crops thrive.

pH7–7.5 Alkaline.
Typical of hot, dry areas.
Most garden plants survive.

pH above 8 Very alkaline,
Typical of semi-desert areas.
Soil life and plants struggle.

Never add slaked lime or hydrated lime as these are very soluble and quick-acting, so you shouldn't use them in an organic garden. The best lime comes from Dolomitic limestone as this contains significant magnesium as well as calcium.

Plants for particular soils

Plants for acid soils
bilberry
cranberry
rhubarb
strawberry
raspberry
tomato
celery
potato
parsnip
red maple
rhododendron
camellia
azaleas
heathers
magnolia
spruce

Plants for alkaline soils
brassica
asparagus
spinach
currant
apple
peach
plum
orchid
fritillary
tulip
holly
beech
cedar
cypress
wisteria
lilac

Plants for sandy soils
onion
carrot
parsnip
beetroot
salad greens
rocket
chard
runner bean
tomato
nasturtium
soft fruit (except
strawberries and
raspberries)
apple
nut trees
sweet chestnut
holm oak
catmint

Plants for clay soils
pea
broad bean
potato
parsley
squash
strawberry
raspberry
pear
plum
rose
willow
oak
black walnut
poplar
dogwood
elder

Soil checklist

	Sand	Clay	Loam	
STRUCTURE	**Sand** Very open; unwilling to form clods. Needs continuous supplies of organic matter. Never leave sandy soil bare, but protect with mulch or green manure when not in cultivation.	**Clay** Tiny particles stick together closely and it needs opening up. Requires grit and well-rotted organic matter.	**Loam** Good structure, which is easy to maintain with regular addition of organic matter.	**STRUCTURE**
DRAINAGE	Swift to drain, but nutrients leach out easily and the soil dries out easily and suffers from drought. Organic matter improves drainage by making the soil more spongy.	Tends to waterlog, causing lack of aeration and stressed plants and soil life. However, holds nutrients well. If it dries out it becomes cement-like and impenetrable, so mulch well in summer.	Drains well, but retains enough moisture to hold nutrients. Not drought-susceptible.	**DRAINAGE**
TEMPERATURE	Warms up quickly, so ideal for early crops.	Cold; not suitable for early crops. Because of the high moisture content it is quick to freeze.	Warms up quite early and slow to freeze, so provides the longest growing seasons.	**TEMPERATURE**
CULTIVATION	Sandy soil can be worked at virtually any time as long as organic matter is always incorporated.	Only ever cultivate clay soil in dry weather. Add very well-rotted organic matter as lack of air means slow decomposition. Turn soil on seed beds in autumn and leave frost to break up the structure.	Do not work in wet; otherwise tolerant.	**CULTIVATION**
pH	Often chalky and alkaline, but check every two years as lime is easily washed out of light, sandy soils.	Clay soil tends to be slightly acid; liming encourages clay particles to clump together in larger groups.	Usually around neutral, but check every five years.	**pH**

	Peat *Good.*	**Silt** *Good.*
STRUCTURE		
DRAINAGE	*The most fertile peat soils drain well, but can dry out into a hard crust; others hold too much water.*	*Silt is a combination of sandy and clay deposits and has some of the characteristics of each. It can pack down and become waterlogged, but it also dries out to a free-draining dust.*
TEMPERATURE	*Quick to warm; slow to freeze.*	*Slow to warm, or to freeze.*
CULTIVATION	*Any time.*	*Cultivate when soil is moist, neither wet nor dry*
pH	*Usually acid; sometimes very acid.*	*Typically neutral to acid.*

Soil deficiencies

nitrogen
Symptoms: pale yellowing foliage, small leaves, stunted growth.
Cure: add muck and compost, improve drainage, rotate crops (see page 89).

phosphorus
Symptoms: small pale leaves, slow growth; leaves have blue-green tinge and fall early.
Cure: add compost, improve drainage.

potassium
Symptoms: pale leaves and stunted growth, brown-tipped leaves with yellow between veins.
Cure: Comfrey tea, rock dust.

magnesium
Symptoms: green-veined mature leaves with yellow between veins.
Cure: Epsom salts, compost.

iron
Symptoms: young leaves yellow between veins.
Cure: reduce pH with liberal compost, sulphur, or gypsum.

manganese
Symptoms: mature leaves fade.
Cure: raise pH – add lime or chalk.

How do I improve my soil?

Learn the best ways to cultivate your soil, what organic fertilisers to add, and how and when to add them. It's not all hard work. You can even choose to build up a healthy soil without touching a spade.

Add Compost

Organic gardeners go on a lot about compost. That's because it's the best organic matter you can give to your soil. It's entirely natural, recycled from your waste products, and free. Garden compost provides your soil with the nutrients and micro-nutrients it needs. It encourages helpful soil organisms while discouraging those that bring disease.

   One of the principles of organic gardening is to try to maintain the fertile cycle of growth and decay by recycling nutrients, importing as little extra material as possible into your garden. The weeds and plants that go into a compost heap have spent their lives gathering minerals as well as nitrogen-rich proteins from your soil. When you return them to the compost heap all these elements are on their way back into the soil. And when you add the finished compost to your soil it then releases its plant foods slowly when they are needed.

   Compost is so crucial to successful organic gardening that the next chapter is dedicated to the subject.

Apply manure

Manure has always been a valuable fertiliser. It provides high levels of nitrogen and also contains a good range of all the other nutrients your soil needs.

   Strawy manure is always best, as much of the goodness in muck comes from the urine, and rotted straw is also a good soil conditioner. Poultry manure is very rich – most useful when added to the compost heap to speed up composting rather than digging it straight into the soil. Well-rotted cow muck is an excellent fertiliser, and it is usually quite easy to come by, but town gardeners may find horse muck more readily available. This is also a good source of nutrients, but avoid muck mixed with wood shavings as the bacteria will spend all their time trying to decompose the sawdust rather than helping the fertility of your soil. Pig muck is good, but be careful of its source – never get it from intensive-rearing systems as the pigs are often fed with copper supplements, which can be toxic to your soil. Sheep and

Never get manure from intensive rearing systems, where extra minerals and medicines are often added to supplement the animals' indoor lifestyle and fast-food diet.

Never use manure fresh on your garden as the high levels of nitrogen can scorch plant roots and harm seed germination. It should always be rotted or composted before use (see page 58).

Don't worry about importing weed seeds in manure. As long as the animals didn't exist entirely on a diet of weeds, and the muck is rotted or composted, you are unlikely to have too much of a problem. Even if you do get a few weeds, it's easier to pull them out than it is to grow plants in infertile soil.

Muck *is full of micro-organisms, which feed soil life and speed up composting processes.*

goat muck is valuable, but less available, and bat droppings are excellent, but hard to find.

Only muck your soil thoroughly every three years or so as it is too nitrogen-rich for some plants and causes sappy growth and weak plants. It is best to apply muck to land about four to six weeks before you plant, or fork it carefully around growing plants, keeping it off their stems.

Dig or no-dig?

Most people assume that digging is an integral part of gardening, but in a properly managed organic garden you should only need to dig your ground once, right at the beginning. Then you need never lift a spade again, if you don't wish to. If you are patient, you don't even need to dig at the beginning, but can cover your ground with a long-term mulch (see page 35) to clear the ground while you get on with other tasks.

However, most gardeners are itching to get at the soil when they take over a garden, to start the work of improving it and creating a fertile patch as soon as possible. You will want to check the condition of the soil and see where improvements need to be made, and to clear unwanted growth from areas you want to plant.

Take as much care as possible to clear the ground thoroughly at this stage, as you do not want to be forced to dig in following years, but you do want to give future plants the best chances of getting at all the available nutrients they need.

DIGGING ADVANTAGES

The prime purpose of digging is to incorporate organic matter along with the air the soil needs for plant roots and soil organisms to breathe. Digging also loosens soils, breaking up heavy clods to allow roots easier penetration, and providing channels for rain water to soak in to the ground. This is very important in a garden that has been neglected, and in gardens on new building developments, where the soil is often very poor-quality topsoil imported and dumped over hardpan. In such conditions, you can add organic matter or other soil improvers (see page 37) when you dig.

Digging brings pests to the surface, where they can provide meals for birds and other predators.

DIGGING DISADVANTAGES

While soil benefits from a good shake up in the right conditions, it doesn't appreciate being trodden on as this compacts it. So if you dig too often, or at the wrong time, you will harm soil structure and soil organisms. Clay needs to be opened up by adding well-rotted organic matter and grit, but it is important that you only work clay when it is dry. If you try to dig when clay is wet, it becomes more solid and sticky.

Heavy clay soil should ideally be dug in autumn, when soil conditions permit, incorporating lots of leafmould (see page 58), and perhaps some grit, and leaving the frosts to help break up the clods into smaller crumbs. It's easy to tell if a clay soil is too wet to dig – your boots will be covered almost as soon as you start. If it is too dry, it will set like concrete and you won't be able to get a spade into it. Even in optimum digging conditions clay soil can be heavy-going, and you certainly won't want to dig it regularly. Once it has been dug over you should continue to open it up by planting green manures (see page 39) and keeping bare areas mulched.

In theory, light sandy soil can be dug in any weather conditions as it does not compact like clay. But if you open it up by digging too much, without adding copious amounts of organic matter sandy soil will become less rather than more nutrient-retentive, losing moisture and organic matter. Never dig a sandy soil in autumn or leave it bare – cover it with a growing crop of green manure or a thick mulch of organic matter.

DIGGING METHODS

There are many methods of digging, but they all aim to do the same job: to aerate and fertilise the soil and leave it in a condition where it needs no further spadework.

To decide your digging strategy, see what you're dealing with by digging a hole about two spade heads, or 'spits', deep. The soil will probably be rather compacted in the top spit, but if it is reasonably loose underneath you can get away with light digging one spit deep, taking out weeds and forking organic matter in as you go.

Whichever tools you choose, make sure to keep them clean and sharp. Dirty tools can spread disease organisms into your soil and blunt tools make for hard work. Always clean your spade or fork after use by knocking off surplus soil and storing it in a sand box, or rub it with sand before hanging it on a wall. You can add a bit of old sump oil to the sand.

Never work soil when it is wet, as digging or treading makes the structure even worse.

If you dig to remove annual weeds, the benefit is short-lived as you will bring nearer the surface the thousands of dormant weed seeds that live in the soil waiting for the right conditions to germinate.

Instead of digging turf into the soil, you can remove it in about a 10-cm layer and stack it, grass-side down. If you water it and keep the pile covered with a polythene sheet, you will have fine loam in a few months, ideal for potting compost or for adding to topsoil. But this seriously robs any bed where the turf came from, so it is best only to stack turf where you are removing it for a path, or similar.

DOUBLE DIGGING

If the soil is compacted at the deeper level you need to loosen it for drainage and aeration or plant roots will never get the nutrients they need. The most successful way to do this is by double digging. Some people get quite fanatical about double digging, but it is not difficult, just rather hard work. It involves turning over the subsoil as well as the topsoil, adding organic matter to each. The only rule is not to mix the levels of subsoil and topsoil.

The best way is to divide the plot to be dug into roughly 45-centimetre squares. Take out a spit of topsoil from the first and second squares and a spit of subsoil from the first square, and leave these to one side. Then take the subsoil from the second square and turn it into the first square, adding compost or manure with it. Cover this with weeded topsoil from the third square, also mixed with organic matter, and so on. The topsoil and subsoil from your starting point ends up in the final squares.

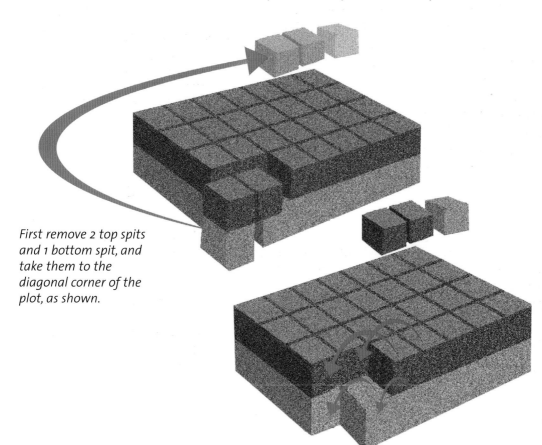

First remove 2 top spits and 1 bottom spit, and take them to the diagonal corner of the plot, as shown.

Then repeat, moving each spit along 1 spit. Make sure to keep the lower spits below the upper spits. If the soil is compacted, work in plenty of compost as you go.

CLEARING GRASS

If you're clearing old turf you can't just turn it over or it will regrow and you'll have endless problems. Instead, use another digging method, called bastard trenching. As you do for double digging (see page 33), keep to your squares and dig two spits deep. Scalp a few centimetres of turf off the top of each square and bury it under soil in the neighbouring square.

ROTOVATING

When you want to cultivate a large area, or clear very weedy soil or rough grass, you may consider using a rotovator. Rotovators have tines that chop up the surface of the soil, and they can perform the equivalent of digging, forking, and breaking down clods. However, you will need to rotovate a patch of ground several times to clear it, as each time you rotovate you will chop up weed roots and potentially spread any that are not left on the surface to dry out. If you go over the ground a few times during the growing season, when the plot greens up, you will eventually weaken the weeds and tough grasses, kill them, and incorporate them into the soil.

Only ever rotovate soil when it is dry, to minimise weed spread. Unless you add generous quantities of organic matter to the soil as you clear it, even in the best conditions rotovating tends to harm the soil structure. If possible, sow a green manure with wide-reaching root spread after rotovating to help restore it.

THE NO-DIG METHOD

The basic principle of the no-digging technique is always to leave a thick layer of well-rotted compost covering the surface of your soil, and to keep renewing it. You just plant your plants in that. Some people never dig their gardens at all. Not even to start. You can create beds without digging in all but heavy clay soil covering the ground with layers of organic matter; earthworms and other organisms should then incorporate it into the soil for you.

Don't overwinter a rotovator on a concrete floor – put it on a board or old pallet to avoid damp and rusting.

Don't mulch very wet soils as this can promote some diseases and increase chances of rot. If spread too thickly, mulches can interfere with aeration of the soil.

One disadvantage of mulch is its other probable role as a slug and snail hotel, providing the warm, moist conditions they love. Be vigilant, especially when you rake off a temporary mulch. On the plus side, it is possible that mulch may also provide slugs and snails with an alternative food source to your plants.

Don't try the no-dig method if you're starting a garden on unimproved, heavy clay soil. Piling compost on top of cold, wet clay would lead to your soil becoming increasingly airless, waterlogged and stale. The lack of aeration in heavy clay inhibits the organisms that break down the organic matter, so you could make a difficult soil worse.

No-dig gardeners need to think ahead when planning their garden as the growing area will be out of action for at least one growing season, preferably longer, to clear the ground. The first step is to mow grass and chop down weeds on the area you want to turn into a productive bed, and water the ground well. Then spread a light-excluding layer of dampened newsprint (around 8 pages thick) or cardboard on the ground. This should prevent weed seeds germinating. Cover this with a 'sheet' of well-rotted organic matter, spreading a layer around 10 centimetres thick to cover the ground completely. Cover this with another layer of moistened newsprint or cardboard to smother any weeds that get through the first layer and cover this with more compost. Keep everything damp so that living organisms can get to work, rotting all the organic matter.

You should be able to plant into the new bed after six months, adding no more than 2 centimetres of well-rotted compost and planting through that. If weeds appear, remove them with a hand fork – don't disturb the bed by digging. Keep topping up with compost in spring and/or autumn.

Mulch

If you want to improve and protect your soil's fertility, mulch. Mulching means covering the ground with a layer of material. It is the easiest way of adding organic matter – just spread the mulch on top of the ground and let worms and other soil creatures do the work of incorporating it into the soil. This will also suppress most weeds by keeping light out.

Mulching keeps the soil moist and prevents it drying out in hot weather; it also prevents soil getting waterlogged in winter. A layer of mulch shades soil, reducing heat stress on plants and soil organisms. It helps the soil temperature to stay reasonably constant, keeps it warmer for longer in autumn to extend the growing season, and insulates it in winter. This regulating effect helps soil structure, plants, and soil life.

When you leave unplanted soil well mulched over winter, this prevents erosion from extreme weather.

MULCHING MATERIALS

The most common mulches are organic materials. Compost, well-rotted strawy muck, grass mowings, or leafmould may be applied as slow-release fertilising mulches. These can also be used to add a protective layer to the soil over winter. If you're short of compost, wetted straw and hay also make good winter protection – a small proportion will get worked into the soil, but rake off the excess in spring to avoid starving the soil of nitrogen.

Woodchips can make an attractive mulch, but leave them in a pile to decay for six months to a year before using or they can tie up enough soil nitrogen to interfere with plant growth. Grit makes an effective mulch for plants that require good drainage, and to keep slugs and snails at bay, but don't use it on sandy soils.

WHEN TO MULCH

Your soil must be fairly wet before you add mulch, as rain water will only trickle slowly through the mulching material and some will be absorbed before it gets to the soil. On the other hand, your soil won't lose much moisture and even in a hot, dry summer it should stay moist a few centimetres beneath the mulch.

Unless you are following the no-dig method, in spring you should fork in or rake off excess winter mulch a few weeks before planting to let soil warm up, and wait to re-mulch perennial plantings until plants put out new growth. Then, mulch well to ensure that soil stays fertile and moist through the summer. In autumn it can pay to rake off excess summer mulch and let birds get at the grubs and pests in the soil. Wait until the first hard frost before you re-cover beds with a thick layer of loose mulch to prevent winter erosion and as good

Leave soil bare for a few weeks in autumn, before spreading winter mulch. This gives birds the chance to dig through the soil and eat pests and pests' eggs and larvae.

Gardeners should steer away from **peat** because of the environmental problems in digging it, but even if you live in an area of plentiful peat, never use it as a mulch. It forms a water-repellent crust that sheds instead of absorbs rain, and if it is left on top of the soil it takes an age to break down. So peat is a poor source of organic matter and nutrients.

From the left, thick black plastic, bark, cardboard or carpet are equally good mulches.

insulation from the thawing and freezing that harms plants. Straw, hay, and chopped bracken make good insulating mulches.

Add other soil improvers

Few gardeners generate enough compost from their own household and garden to keep their soil in best condition. Fortunately plenty of other materials are widely available.

GRASS CLIPPINGS

Lawn mowings are best left on the lawn, or composted, but they also make a good mulch on sandy soils, and an excellent nitrogen boost for potatoes if you lay them straight into potato trenches. Never leave a thick layer of fresh grass clippings on top of clay soil as they will rob the soil of nitrogen while they decompose, or turn to slime and further prevent aeration of the soil.

LEAFMOULD

Autumn leafmould (see page 58) is not a fertiliser as it contains scarcely any plant foods, but it adds bulky organic matter to condition soil, and makes excellent weed-suppressant mulch. The easiest way to collect autumn leaves from a lawn is to run the mower over them with the grass box on. This chops the leaves and mixes them with grass clippings, which will speed their decay. Otherwise rake them up when they are damp and either pile them into a heap and cover it with polythene, or put small quantities into loosely tied plastic sacks. Leave them for at least six months before digging them into your soil or using as mulch.

SEAWEED

The unrestricted use of seaweed, either fresh or calcified, to reduce soil acidity, is not recommended by the Soil Association. Taking fresh seaweed from the shore damages the natural ecosystem of the beach and endangers certain seaweed species. Calcified seaweed is a restricted product for organic growers and farmers. Ground limestone or chalk should be used as an alternative.

COMFREY

Everyone should grow comfrey as a mineral-rich fertiliser. This deep-rooted plant is low in fibre and high in protein, the best source of

A bed of comfrey is invaluable as both fertiliser and green manure.

potassium for organic gardeners, and contains significant levels of nitrogen and phosphorus. It grows faster than any other plant in your garden so you can crop stems and leaves every six weeks through the growing season. No pests will attack your comfrey plants.

Cut comfrey stems and leaves and wilt them for one or two days before digging them straight into the soil. Comfrey also makes an excellent summer mulch around tomatoes and bush fruit, adding fertility and deterring pests and diseases. However, don't use comfrey on acid-loving plants.

MUSHROOM COMPOST

Organic mushroom compost is an excellent soil conditioner, fertiliser, and mulch, as long as it is based on well-rotted manure. However, much commercial mushroom compost contains pesticide residues as well as high levels of lime. Leave it in a pile under cover for six months before using it, and don't use it on acid-loving plants.

OTHER CONDITIONERS

Hoof and horn provides slow release of nitrogen, bonemeal provides calcium and phosphorus; both are good general fertilisers to build strong root growth, but check there are no chemical additives used in the sterilising process. Blood, fish, and bone also makes a good spring tonic to get growth off to a good start. It releases nitrogen fast and other elements, including trace elements, more slowly.

If you want to make a seed bed in spring on clay soil, mulch it with well-rotted compost or leafmould over the winter, and rake off excess in spring. You won't be able to dig a mulch into clay soil until late in spring because of the difficulty in cultivating clay soils, except in dry weather, when the soil is not wet.

In some areas recycled municipal waste is available. Although this is of variable quality, it can be a good source of bulky organic matter, and far better to get garden supplements from a local source than imported. Some local authorities compost grass-mowings. Many have schemes to recycle shredded prunings. Others provide composted humanure. Ask about the content of what is available.

Peat is no longer recommended because of concerns about the environmental impact of its extraction.

Hair, fur, wool, and feathers all release nitrogen slowly. Either compost or dig them into the soil in autumn.

Grow green manures

Green manures are fast-growing crops that you grow for the primary purpose of turning them into the soil to add organic matter. They are sometimes known as 'cover crops' or 'living compost'. When the crop is mature, and before it flowers, you dig it in to the ground or cut it and leave it on top of the soil as a mulch for the worms to incorporate into your soil.

Green manures improve soils in several ways. They prevent weeds colonising bare soil; they increase biological activity in the soil; they help to prevent pests and diseases from establishing themselves; and they add bulky organic matter.

Even a small patch of green manure is effective. It is most often used in the vegetable patch, both as a way of improving the soil when you start your garden, and as part of your rotation plan (see page 89). If you leave an area of soil bare, nutrients in the soil will be carried away by wind, rain, or even heat; nitrogen will be lost in ammonia gas; and harsh weather can damage soil structure. But if a green manure crop is growing, plant moisture and nourishment will stay in the soil, and its structure will be improved rather than eroded by weather conditions.

In a small garden, you're most likely to want a winter-growing green manure to cover resting soil. In a larger garden, summer green manures are useful if you don't want to cultivate the whole area, particularly to suppress weeds and bolster fertility as part of your rotation system.

Legumes and grasses are the most common green manures. Legumes include peas and beans, clovers, and alfalfa. They can fix nitrogen from the air in their root nodules and return it to the soil. Turning legumes into the soil at any growth stage adds organic matter and improves soil life.

Grasses provide dense cover with good root penetration; they are particularly valuable for weed control and to improve structure. Many grasses have extensive root systems. When the roots decay they leave not only organic matter

Below, Phacelia (Phacelia tanacetifolia) is an attractive summer green manure, ideal for the garden, with lavender-blue flowers that bees and other insects love. It will also withstand a mild winter.

but also hundreds of fine channels in the soil. So they aerate the soil and improve drainage.

Some legumes, notably alfalfa, but also clovers, have deep root systems, reaching right down to take nutrients from the subsoil. When the plants decompose, these nutrients are returned to the topsoil, where even shallow-rooted plants can use them.

WINTER COVER

Winter tares are one of the few hardy legumes. When sown in late summer they will grow until well into the winter and stand until spring, when you can cut them down and dig them in as nitrogen-rich compost. Phacelia and crimson clover will also survive mild winters.

Many summer green manures also attract beneficial insects into your garden. Buckwheat is an excellent summer weed suppressor and bulky green manure. It will grow on very poor soil, and hoverflies love it.

Winter tares

Clovers suitable for green manuring perform best on light soils.

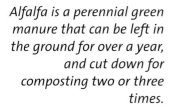

Alfalfa is a perennial green manure that can be left in the ground for over a year, and cut down for composting two or three times.

Comfrey grown as green manure

The best **comfrey** for gardeners is a variety called Bocking 14, selected by the Henry Doubleday Research Association (HDRA) from varieties imported from Russia. It is a hybrid of common comfrey (*Symphytum officinale*) and prickly comfrey (*Symphytum asperum*) and is sometimes known as Russian comfrey. It can be used as a quick-rotting mulch, but not on flowering plants.

Improve drainage

Drainage problems may be caused by poor soil structure and can be fixed by adding organic matter and building up the fertility of your soil. But sometimes you may need to find other solutions.

POOR DRAINAGE

When the water table is near the surface or the subsoil is heavy clay or rock, soil will get waterlogged – plants and soil-living organisms will not be able to get enough oxygen and soil will stagnate. If double digging, green manuring and adding organic matter fail to solve the problem, you could take advantage of the conditions to create a bog garden of plants that love these conditions. But if you want a wider choice of plants you will have to make drains.

To effectively drain large areas, you may need to lay underground drainage pipes (see figure 1). Rubble drains are the simplest do-it-yourself drains for a small plot (see figure 2). Dig a trench 60–90 cm deep and 30 cm wide, with a gentle slope of about 1 in 30, preferably leading to a ditch or drain. Half-fill it with rubble, top with gravel and replace the topsoil. If there is nowhere for your drain to go you will need to dig a soakaway – a hole at least 1.5m wide and deep, lined with bricks, filled with rubble and topped with turf. You should dig your drainage trenches by hand as even a small excavator will further compact your soil and add to fertility problems.

1 A traditional herringbone pattern of loosely jointed clay pipes should always run downhill and feed into a ditch or soakaway.

2 These cross sections are filled with (a) clay pipe and rubble, (b) clay pipe, (c) trenches just filled with rubble or (d) faggots. All trenches are topped with soil turf.

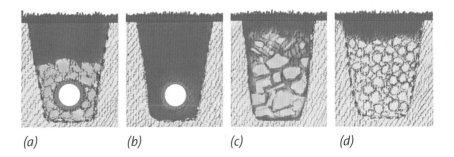

(a)   *(b)*   *(c)*   *(d)*

compost

waste becomes wealth

compost

Everyone should recycle, and gardeners can recycle more than most. Anything that was once plant or animal matter can be composted and returned to the soil that originally nourished it, providing nutrition for new generations of both plants and animals.

There was a time when all gardeners composted; when waste had to be recycled because there was nothing else you could do with it. If you kept chickens or pigs, vegetable scraps, and garden waste were fed to the animals, their muck was then put in a heap, left to rot, and spread on the garden to feed the plants. If you didn't keep animals, anything that would rot was put in a pile and later distributed over the garden; other materials were burnt and the resulting ash was then put on the garden. Gardeners provided all the nutrition their garden needed from the home and garden. They naturally looked after the soil and the planet, using available resources wisely.

RECYCLING MATERIAL

Nowadays we don't have to recycle, we can choose to have our waste taken away to landfill sites. We don't have to think about the amount of waste we produce because we don't have to deal with it ourselves. Around 60 per cent of domestic waste is organic matter, and much of the other 40 per cent is packaging.

When you compost you not only reduce your waste output, lessening the problem of using tracts of land for waste disposal, at the same time you reduce the need to bring materials in from outside to enrich your garden. You won't need extra fertilisers or composts if you

Compost is a mixture of organic materials such as weeds, grass mowings, garden waste, and kitchen scraps, which decay into a dark crumbly mass, often called humus. It improves your soil, provides a balanced diet of nutrients for your soil and plants, it's easy to make, and it's free.

You don 't have to have a large garden, you can compost kitchen scraps in a worm bin on a balcony if that's your situation; you can be a lazy composter or a manically enthusiastic one; you can follow strict rules or more or less make them up as you go along, once you know how the process works. It's up to you – composting is not an exact science. There's a good deal of trial and error. It depends on your time and energy, the food that you eat and the plants that you grow.

When you add compost to your soil you add healthy soil life and help to control harmful bacteria and fungi, keeping soil and plants disease-free.

can make your own. One of the principles of organic gardening is to be as self-sufficient as possible in the materials you need, avoiding the use of energy on transport and processing. When you compost you fulfil this principle.

Garden compost is the best material for feeding your soil. When you recycle organic matter into your soil you are returning plants and tiny living creatures that once came from it, in the form of minerals, proteins, carbohydrates, and sugars. These provide the nutrients plants and animals need to grow, then they in turn die, decay, and provide more food for future generations. So you are helping to maintain the cycle of fertility.

Helping nature

Whenever a plant or animal dies and falls to the ground it will eventually rot down and ultimately return to the soil. Leaves and twigs, for example, fall, rot, and feed the tree above with nutrients that once came from the tree. So why don't we just leave vegetation to compost itself?

For one thing, few gardeners would like to have rotting bits of vegetation all around the place. More important is that organic matter is rotted by the action of tiny organisms, and if they come across a chunk of unrotted material in or on the soil they take nutrients from the soil to help them decompose it. So every time they have to get to work to rot something down into a form where it can be reintegrated into the soil, they are temporarily robbing the soil of elements that it needs to feed plants.

When the processes are confined to a compost heap they are altogether more efficient. Composting also mixes different materials, so you end up with a wide spread of balanced elements, rather than concentration of a few, and the composted plant foods are stored and released slowly into the soil when they are needed.

What is composting?

It's very simple, but it seems like magic. You throw all your kitchen and garden rubbish onto a heap, add a bit of muck and maybe one or two extras, and tiny creatures convert it into crumbly sweet-smelling stuff that plants can feed from as and when they need it.

Your compost heap is not just a pile of old waste, but a teeming pile of life and energy: macro-organisms and micro-organisms,

If you dig garden rubbish directly into the soil you can cause a reduction rather than increase in yield. Young and sappy stuff can be dug in because it breaks down fast, but old stemmy materials will rob the soil of essential nitrogen as bacteria break it down.

If you don't make enough – buy it
If you don't generate enough waste materials to make as much compost as you need, buy more ready-made. Many local councils sell recycled municipal waste, ranging from leafmould to manure. It may not have the wide range of nutrients that good home-made garden compost will contain, but suppliers will be able to tell you exactly what the compost contains so you can decide how best to use it.

chemical processes and physical ones, reproduction, death, new life... it's a seething hotbed of activity.

As soon as you lay down some organic material into a compost pile organisms get to work. All organic matter contains substances that plants need to grow, but these remain locked up until transformed by decomposing organisms into compounds that plants can absorb.

Macro-organisms include mites, centipedes, millipedes, spiders, springtails, beetles, ants, flies, nematodes, and earthworms. They start the work of decomposing, dragging materials through the heap, and chewing, grinding, sucking, and tearing them into smaller pieces. The smaller the pieces, the larger the surface area for the micro-organisms – bacteria and fungi – to get at. These then digest whatever they come across, liberating nutritious elements locked into the waste.

BACTERIA

The bacteria in compost heaps depend on the material, temperature, moisture, and air content. Bacteria produce enzymes to digest whatever organic material is available to them. The most important bacteria are psychrophiles, mesophiles, and thermophiles. As they feed on the waste they break down compounds, grow and multiply and release heat as a by-product. The problem for bacteria is that they kill themselves off – as they work and reproduce they make their environment too hot to live in, so they die or move to cooler areas at the edge of the heap.

Psychrophiles, or low-temperature bacteria, start things off in colder situations. They operate at cool temperatures, below 15°C. As they consume fibrous matter they oxidise carbon and raise the heat of the heap so the next level of bacteria can get to work. In very cool areas psychrophiles will do most of the work, so the composting process can take over a year.

Mesophilic bacteria are medium-temperature operators, content (like humans) at between 15°C–40°C. If you start a compost pile in summer, mesophiles will get straight in there. In most compost piles mesophiles do the bulk of the bacterial work, but if they generate too much heat their job is finished. In hotter temperatures, over 40°C, thermophiles or high-temperature operators take over. They can take the temperature right up to 75°C. They are the shortest-lived of all the composting bacteria as a heap shouldn't remain too hot too long.

Micro-organisms in the compost heap need carbon (C), nitrogen (N), phosphorus (P) and potassium (K) to make the enzymes that transform matter into the humus that feeds plants. So a compost heap should contain a variety of materials.

Compost needs air so that **aerobic** bacteria can get to work. Most materials will eventually decay through anaerobic decomposition, but this is more akin to putrefaction, where air is largely excluded. An anaerobic heap will smell unpleasant and resulting compost will be slimy and hard to integrate, although it will break down eventually. Keep a heap aerated by mixing materials well or turning occasionally.

All organic matter contains carbohydrates and proteins. During composting, carbohydrates (starches and sugars) break down to simple sugars, organic acids, and carbon dioxide to be released in the soil. Proteins decompose into peptides and amino acids, then to available ammonium compounds and atmospheric nitrogen. Ammonium compounds are changed by nitrifying bacteria into nitrates supplying soil nitrogen.

It is not **heat** itself that breaks down organic matter, but the process of heating is created by specific bacteria that create the conditions for different strains of organisms to carry on the work of efficient decomposing.

In the right conditions **thermophiles** should be able to do all their highest temperature work within a week. If a heap stays too hot for too long some vital elements can be damaged – for example, nitrogen will be given off as ammonia gas and the temperature will need to be lowered by turning the heap or aerating it.

You can check to see how composting is coming along by looking for signs of actinomycetes – cobwebby structures around fibres in the heap. If these are plentiful you know the decomposing process is doing fine. As actinomycetes increase in a compost pile they produce antibiotics that inhibit bacterial growth.

Poultry can form an important part of the cycle of fertility, scratching around for food and donating manure and feathers.

ACTINOMYCETES AND FUNGI

Well-made compost has a characteristic earthy smell, like newly turned soil or freshly picked mushrooms. This is caused by actinomycetes at work. They are a higher form of bacteria that increase as decomposition gets under way. They liberate carbon, nitrogen, and ammonia from decomposing matter. Fungi also take over at the later stages of decomposition, breaking down complicated compounds and releasing further nutrients.

What does compost do to my soil?

When you add compost to your soil you increase fertility by improving the soil structure, so that it can accept and use nutrients effectively. You also provide those nutrients.

In good garden soils, the particles stick together in an assortment of large and small crumbs. But in light, sandy soils large particles refuse to join together, so air and water and nutrients drain away between them. While in heavy, clay soils the particles are so tiny that they fuse together in sticky clods so air and water can't get through. Incorporating compost can correct both problems, lightening and aerating a heavy soil, and making a light one more spongy and absorbent.

The water content is particularly crucial to soil. It should never be allowed either to get too wet or too dry, because plants can't get at the air, moisture or food they need, and soil life suffers with potentially harmful bacteria taking the place of beneficial ones. Compost soaks up water like a sponge – 100 pounds of humus can hold 195 pounds of water – then releases it slowly, so soil into which plenty of compost has been incorporated withstands drought, but should never become waterlogged.

Compost adds life to your soil, adding micro-organisms and larger creatures such as earthworms and insects that are nature's soil-builders. The more life in your soil, the better the structure, and the higher the nutrient levels.

Compost contains all the major elements – nitrogen (N), phosphorus (P), and potassium (K) – that plants need for optimum growth, as well as the necessary trace elements. It is also an important source of carbon dioxide for plant growth, as the organisms in compost give off carbon dioxide when they breathe.

The most fantastic thing about compost is that it releases nutrients gradually when plants most need them, throughout the growing season. It works with the soil. When soil temperatures are low – when plants are young in spring and at early growth stages, or slowing down for the winter – compost releases nutrients slowly, but as soil temperatures heat up and plants move into a stage of rapid growth the micro-organisms in the compost and the soil work harder and release more plant food.

Compost improves the ability of soil to retain appropriate levels of water. Plants grown in compost-rich soil can access all the air, moisture, and nutrients they need.

MICRONUTRIENTS

Although micronutrients – iron, cobalt, manganese, boron, zinc, molybdenum, and iodine – are needed by plants in minute quantities, they are still vital to plant growth and reproduction. Many soils may show signs of deficiencies, but high levels also harm plant growth. It is hard to feed the soil with a specific trace element, in a form that plants can use, without running the risk of building up excess levels and therefore potential toxicity. But compost contains and releases the elements when plants need them.

Almost all soils contain enough micronutrients, but they may be inaccessible. In very alkaline soils, iron, copper, and manganese, for example, get locked up in insoluble compounds. But if there is enough compost in the soil, the trace elements will remain available in solution. The other extreme can occur in acid soils, where you often find an excess of trace elements in solution, sometimes at levels which are toxic to plants. Compost is also able to mop up this excess and store extra elements away to be called on when needed.

As plants grow they gather the minerals of their choice from the soil. When they are composted at the end of their life they return these materials to the soil to be dispersed.

Humic acids produced in composting can pull nutrients out of minerals already in the soil and make them available to plants.

The nutrients in compost are also needed by soil organisms which, in turn, provide plants with more nutrients.

The more varied the composting materials you use, the greater variety of nutrients your compost will contain.

What can I compost?

You can compost virtually anything that is animal or vegetable matter: if it lived once, it will recycle into nutrients for micro-organisms and plants. You don't need to worry too much about including all the different plant nutrients in your compost pile. If you incorporate a good variety of materials, the necessary nutrients will be there.

HOME COMPOST

From the kitchen you can compost all food scraps apart from meat and fat. The smaller the pieces, the quicker they decompose, and you'll need to chop tough corn cobs, very woody vegetable scraps, and old whole citrus fruits. Tea leaves and coffee grounds are excellent, as are eggshells and crushed seafood shells. If you cover or bury all cooked food scraps you won't run much risk of vermin visiting your heap. If this is a concern, don't compost cooked material.

Old flowers can be added, along with their water, which can contain useful bacteria and moisten the heap. Old aquarium water is also a good addition to moisten the heap as it contains algae and other nutrients that can be recycled. Paper towels and napkins go into compost, along with cardboard tubes – tear them up a bit first. Newspapers will also compost, but they should be shredded and soaked, then mixed in well – don't leave them in a layer or they will compact, go slimy, and stop aerobic bacteria working. Empty your dustpan and vacuum cleaner onto your compost heap. House dust is largely mites, hair, and earth, all of which add to the nutrition in your heap. You can also add woodash, but fairly sparingly as it can make a compost heap too alkaline. Any natural fibre products can be composted, chopping large items up small. Feathers from pillows and mattresses, woollen and cotton clothing, and even leather items will all compost successfully and add nutrition to your heap.

Most animal wastes can go into compost – poultry manure, rabbit or guinea-pig bedding as well as muck from larger animals. But don't add dog or cat excrement, unless you become an expert composter, as these can carry diseases that will only be killed in an efficient hot heap. Human urine is a superb addition.

Just about any waste material from the garden should head for your compost. Weeds, soft prunings, mowings, leaves, even obnoxious perennial weeds such as couch grass and ground elder, if they are dried first, and most weed seeds will be killed by composting. Chop or

Coffee grounds and tea leaves are very high in nitrogen, also relatively high in phosphorus and potassium. Coffee grounds are slightly acidic.

Egg shells contain high levels of nitrogen and phosphorus, and significant potassium.

Banana peel is high in phosphorus, potassium, calcium, magnesium, and sulphur.

Citrus wastes are also very high in phosphorus and potassium.

Grass clippings are one of the main suppliers of nitrogen in a compost heap. Add them in thin layers, alternating with kitchen and garden waste and other bulky material to avoid them matting.

Seven pounds of hair contains as much nitrogen as 100 pounds of manure. Moisten it well and mix with aerating material.

Woollen waste and feathers are high in nitrogen. They need to be moistened well before adding.

shred woody prunings. You can compost diseased stems and leaves as the organisms should be killed by proper composting, but if in doubt burn them, along with thorny and evergreen prunings, and compost the woodash.

A GOOD RATIO

A traditional rule of thumb is to make compost from three parts' vegetable matter to one part animal. Animal waste keeps available nitrogen high in your heap, but if you have lots of grass mowings and leguminous waste you need less muck. Unless you keep poultry and several pets you will probably bring in extra manure. Strawy poultry muck is the best rich addition to compost, followed by cow, horse, pig, and sheep. Never add wet muck as it delays decomposition. Always try and find manure mixed with straw because much of the benefit of muck comes from the urine content; don't use sawdust litter as this takes ages to break down into useful nutrients because of the high carbon/nitrogen ratio (see page 62).

Grow your own compost

If you get keen on composting and want to import as little extra material as possible, grow some plants specially for your compost pile. Or include living compost in areas of your garden.

CUT AND COMPOST

Sunflowers make excellent bulk for a compost heap; particularly worth growing if you have quantities of grass mowings to compost as the sunflowers add valuable bulk, aerate the heap, and are extremely high in fibre to balance protein-rich grass mowings.

Marigolds (*Tagetes minuta*) are also worth growing for compost. While they grow they act as effective pest deterrents – particularly for soil pests such as eelworm – and also prevent weed growth because of the enzymes they produce. When you pull them for compost you add valuable bulk to your heap.

Comfrey is in a class of its own. Its strong roots can dig as deep as 2 metres to gather vital minerals, which are made available to other plants when comfrey leaves are composted. Not only is it a great soil improver (see page 37), it also gets compost going (see page 57), is an important source of potassium for organic gardeners, and grows so quickly you can crop the leaves every six weeks or so. Sturdy perennial plants last many years.

Woodash is high in potassium, but use sparingly in the garden as it is very alkaline. Keep woodash away from clay soils as it contains salts that can interfere with their structure and harm fertility.

Straw is good for bulk and aeration, but keep it wet and use in thin layers or it can slow composting by temporarily robbing the heap of nitrogen. Combine with manure for most efficient composting.

Leaves contain high levels of many minerals, but little nitrogen; shred them and use in thin layers in a compost heap, but compost large quantities separately.

Pine needles break down slowly into acidic compost, so add sparingly unless making compost for acid-loving plants.

Seaweed has more potassium than manure but less nitrogen and phosphorus. It contains most trace elements and is a valuable addition to compost.

Green bracken makes excellent bulk, and contains high levels of potassium and nitrogen, and significant phosphorus.

Sunflowers are easy to grow, quick to mature and shade out weeds in the process. Pick them for compost before they flower, before the stems get too thick and hard to chop for compost. Ideally, gather plants less than 1.2m tall, as soon as the first buds show. Just pull them up, knock off as much soil as possible and lay them in your compost heap with grass mowings and other material.

Compost activators

A compost activator kick-starts or speeds up the process of composting. It is a material that encourages biological activity in the heap. Activators such as young nettle plants increase the nitrogen and micro-nutrient content of the heap, providing extra food for micro-organisms. Others such as humus-rich garden soil introduce organisms that break down raw organic matter.

When you are starting a new compost heap it's a good idea to add an activator fairly near the bottom of the pile, then add more at regular intervals. Some people swear by a layer of compost from a recently finished heap, or a layer of good topsoil. Thin (5cm–10cm) layers of nitrogen-rich grass mowings are popular, or strawy muck from a poultry house.

Manure is a rich source of plant nutrients and bacteria, but always partially dry it first as very wet muck will slow down the initial composting process rather than getting it moving. Human urine is an excellent activator because it contains plenty of nitrogen and loses potency less quickly than most animal manures. If there's a baby in the house empty the potty on the heap regularly, and young boys rarely need encouragement to pee straight onto it.

Comfrey and seaweed are dynamic accumulators, which means they collect and store vast amounts of nutrients, and they decompose swiftly to activate your compost. Horsetail also helps speed composting activity – either chop it up (don't add the roots) or leave the hollow stalks to rot slowly, so adding aeration to your heap.

A few handfuls of blood or bonemeal between compost layers speed up decomposition, but may attract dogs and some rodents to cool heaps (see page 65).

Once the organisms in your compost get to work you only need to provide regular supplies of varied materials for the processes to continue.

Leafmould and muck heaps

LEAVES

Although you can add autumn leaves to your compost heap for bulk, don't add too many at once because they contain almost no nitrogen and break down very slowly. It is best to rot them on their own into crumbly leafmould, which releases nutrients very slowly, makes a superb mulch and soil conditioner, and can be used as a base for potting compost.

For a small quantity of leaves you can just scoop them, wet, into black polythene bags, where they will rot down into useable leafmould. The decaying process doesn't need oxygen as it is carried out by fungi whose spores exist on all dead leaves. But if you have leaves in quantity, make leafmould in special-purpose enclosures made of wire netting around sturdy poles up to 1.5 metres tall.

Rake leaves into the enclosures and when you have a sizeable pile, wet and trample them to compact them, then add more. When your pile of leaves is up to the top of the wire, water the leaves further and forget about them for a year or so. If you have space you can leave the leafmould to develop for several years.

MANURE

Manure is an important addition to the compost heap, but let most muck rot separately rather than reducing its bulk through composting.

Either leave small quantities to rot inside a black plastic sack, tied at the neck to keep air out, or make a manure heap. You don't want this to heat up too much or it gets invaded by 'fire-fang' fungus, which destroys nutrients. So compact muck as much as possible to restrict air then cover the heap tightly with polythene. As the manure heats up and ferments, steam will condense and drip back onto the manure to cool it down. The muck will be rotted ready for use within two to three months.

Build a manure heap on ground that you later want to cultivate. Significant nutrients will leach from the manure into the ground as it rots.

For faster results you can add 25 per cent volume of grass mowings to your leafmould piles after six months. Three or four months later you will have useable leafmould.

Well-rotted manure has the carbon/nitrogen ratio of good compost and can be used on its own as fertiliser or as compost activator.

Composting materials

Get going with swift-rotting activators

Grass cuttings

Poultry manure

Comfrey leaves

Pigeon manure

Young weeds

Bat droppings

Nettle leaves and plants

Urine

Horsetail

Keep going with regular supplies

Fruit and vegetable scraps

Eggshells, tea bags, and coffee grounds

Vegetable plant remains – even diseased plants can be composted if your heap heats up

Well-rotted strawy manure

Straw and hay – these rot slowly

Young hedge clippings and soft prunings

Hair and feathers

Shredded woolly jumpers and cotton socks

Hamster, guinea pig, and rabbit bedding and droppings

Old plants

Old cut flowers – purchased flowers can be very high in pesticide residues

Vacuum/dustpan contents

Pond weed

Slow-rotting (add in moderation)

Corncobs – chop up well

Cabbage stems – chop well

Cardboard

Paper bags

Cardboard tubes and egg boxes

Woodash

Autumn leaves

Tough hedge clippings

Woody prunings

Sawdust

Wood shavings

What does compost need?

All composting methods are designed to meet the needs of the organisms and micro-organisms that decompose organic matter. They need a varied diet that is balanced in protein and fibre – nitrogen and carbon – and they need air, moisture, and warmth.

Air

If there's insufficient air in your heap, aerobic bacteria and soil organisms will die off, but there are plenty of ways to keep a compost heap well aerated. You can simply introduce air by turning your pile regularly; the more frequently you turn it, the quicker materials will break down. But this is not always practical, particularly in a sizeable heap, so you'll need to look at other methods.

Maximum aeration usually means fastest decomposition, so if you are at all impatient you'll need to keep helping your heap. You can place layers of pipes or thin poles at intervals through a heap and take them out as the compost gradually heats, or use organic matter for the same job. The soft centres of sunflower stalks rot away quickly to leave hollow tubes, so keep some stalks whole and layer them through the heap every 20 centimetres or so. Jerusalem artichoke stalks do the same job.

BUILDING AIR CIRCULATION

Some composters build off the ground, with wire mesh at the base, collecting any liquids that drip through and recycling them into the container, but it is much better to build a compost heap on the ground so that soil organisms can get straight in. In this case start with a layer of branches and twigs around 15 centimetres deep. This will be slower to decompose than softer materials above and will allow some air to circulate from below. Keep materials in the heap above fairly well shredded so the mass doesn't pack down too tightly and make air circulation difficult.

Moisture

Good compost should be slightly damp, like a wrung-out sponge. If the heap is too dry decomposition will be slow and the heap won't heat up. But if it's too wet air will be driven out of the heap, organisms won't be able to work, and you'll end up with an anaerobic, smelly mess with most nutrients washed away.

If space allows, turning your heap regularly will speed up the process.

Old carpets are perfect for keeping off excess rain and keeping in warmth.

The trick is not to add too much wet or dry material to your heap at any one time. Always leave very wet stuff like farmyard manure or fresh grass mowings to dry slightly before it goes on the heap, and mix any wet kitchen scraps well into the heap. Dry materials such as hay and straw should be chopped or shredded then watered well before you add them.

If your heap gets a bit wet you can mix in dry straw to take up the excess moisture – dried grass clippings are also absorbent. If it tends to dry out, moisten it with water (or urine which also speeds composting), or with compost, manure, or leaf tea (see page 106).

Protect a heap from excessive rain water by covering it. Polythene is fine as long as it doesn't touch the heap; you can also remove it every so often to be moistened by light rain. Cardboard or old carpet are fine if you don't mind their appearance. A thick covering layer of hay makes good insulation as well as a good water repellent. Don't leave your finished compost uncovered or all those hard-won plant nutrients can leach out.

Warmth

Even cold temperature bacteria will be reluctant to get to work if temperatures drop below 13°C, so your heap needs to be well sited and reasonably insulated. Don't put it in an exposed area or where it is subject to crosswinds, and if in doubt you'll need to cover it well and insulate it with a straw bale surround, or similar. Insulation will also help prevent the heap from drying out.

The size of your heap will determine how well it keeps its temperature. If it is too small the heat released by organisms will disappear quickly and it will never reach optimum temperatures; if it is too large it will take ages for you to get finished compost and the outer edges will stay cool. An ideal size for most home composting is at least 1 metre square. If a heap this size is properly built and insulated (see page 69) bacteria should keep on working, even in freezing weather, as they will maintain the internal temperature.

Carbon/nitrogen ratio

If you provide your composting organisms with plenty of material, air, water, and warmth, you should have no problems. But you also need to keep an eye on the proportions of fibre-to-protein that you add. Decomposers need carbon (from fibre) for energy, and nitrogen for protein. If there is too much nitrogen in the pile, then it is released as ammonia or other gases from the breakdown of the proteins in which it is stored. If there is too much carbon, it will take a population explosion of bacteria to decompose it, and they will use up available nitrogen for their own development, causing a shortage. They'll give it back eventually, when they die, but in the meantime nitrogen starvation means uneven decomposition. The same starvation can also occur in the soil when you dig in living compost or fibrous mulches. Well-rotted matter is easily assimilated.

Garden and household waste will probably initially have an average carbon/nitrogen ratio of about 60:1 compared to the 10:1 of fertile soil. If the fibre seems to be breaking down very slowly, add materials with a lower C/N ratio to speed up the process; but if the materials reduce too fast, add bulk with a higher ratio.

Hot composting

Advantages:
Finished compost fast
Efficient use of space
Kills disease organisms
Kills weed seeds

Disdvantages:
High maintenance
Balance of materials crucial
Need to add materials all at once

Carbon/nitrogen ratio

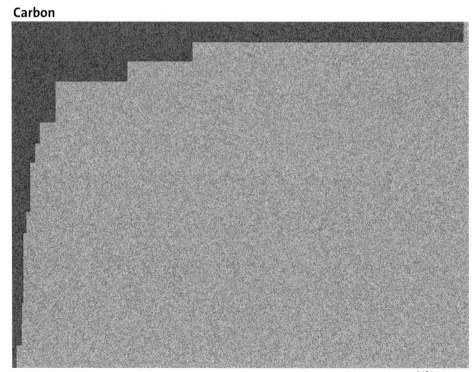

Carbon

Fresh sawdust	500:1
Old sawdust	200:1
Wheatstraw	125:1
Oatstraw	48:1
Bracken	48:1
Young weeds	30:1
Carrots	27:1
Beetroot tops	19:1
Seaweed	19:1
Rotted farmyard manure	14:1
Tomato leaves	12:1
Cabbage greens	12:1
Grassmowings	12:1
Good garden compost	10:1
Comfrey leaves	9.8:1
Dried blood	4:1

Nitrogen

Few gardeners produce enough compost for all their needs.

For maximum production choose hot composting, where you can produce up to six batches a year.

You can also ask non-gardening neighbours to provide you with their organic waste materials.

You can build a compost heap straight over an area that you are going to cultivate. When you remove the finished compost you leave an area rich in soil life and nutrients from the heap. Or you can spread the compost from the heap straight where it is needed.

Making compost

There is a composting method to suit everyone. First, you need to think about how much waste material you produce in your home and garden, how much space you have, how much compost you need, how much time you can give, and how organised you are. There's no point in setting yourself up to maintain a fairly complicated method if you have a haphazard approach to living or if you can only spend time in your garden sporadically.

Most gardeners will probably go for a cool heap, or even just bury waste materials. If you're very tidy you'll probably want a neat container. If you need to see quick results, or you like a technical challenge, you'll probably choose a hot composting method.

Don't be put off composting because you don't produce much waste – even one person's kitchen scraps can feed a worm bin to provide small quantities of highly nutritious plant food.

Hot or cold?

The varied methods of producing compost offer different advantages to the gardener. The main difference between all composting techniques is the speed at which useable compost is produced. Hot heaps work very fast and efficiently and can transform waste into useable compost inside two months. Cool composting methods take longer and are most suitable where you don't need too much compost, or where you have room to make several heaps.

There are also flipsides to each method: hot heaps can take a lot of work and although they destroy weed seeds and diseased material they heat up so much that disease-suppressing microbes are also destroyed in the process. This means when you use the compost it may not be as effective against diseases as that made by other methods. Hot heaps also need to be constructed all at once: you can't just put kitchen waste out as you generate it, but have to store it while you build up enough materials to make an entire heap. And when the heap is constructed you have to keep a close eye on it and turn it every few days, which isn't practical for everyone. Hot composting is also less forgiving than cool – if the heap is too wet or too dry, or if the carbon/nitrogen ratio is out of balance you may have to make adjustments. However, you can safely compost even tough and diseased plant material, and the end result is very even-textured crumbly compost – fast.

Cool heaps don't guarantee to kill disease organisms, and tougher materials may have to be composted more than once. As weed seeds may survive the process, the finished compost may be slightly weedy and tends to have a rather uneven texture, probably containing material at different stages of decay. But weeds are easily pulled out and semi-rotted lumps can be put back in the pile for another go. You can add materials gradually to a cool heap as you gather them, and as long as you keep an eye on the balance of materials to keep everything moist and reasonably aerated your heap should need virtually no maintenance. Also, the finished compost is likely to contain a wider range of living organisms than hot compost.

Where do I put my compost heap?

While you probably won't want your compost heap to be the focus of your view from the house, gone are the days when it had to be hidden away. Other considerations are much more important. If most of your waste comes from the house and kitchen, you should put a cool compost pile somewhere easily accessible from the house. If you're constructing a hot heap, this is less important as you'll need to gather bucketsful of material at one time rather than making regular trips. If the bulk of your waste comes from your garden, make sure your pile is somewhere with easy wheelbarrow access. If you're bringing in manure and other material from elsewhere, it's helpful if you can get a car somewhere nearby.

Don't site your heap where it is in a permanent draught or in deep shade or it will be hard to maintain its moisture and temperature. For the same reasons you don't want it in direct sun either. Ideally it should be protected on the north, east, and west sides by some kind of wall or barrier, and open to the sun on the south. It is best to make a compost heap on the ground, so that earthworms and other organisms can get to work as soon as possible – this is another reason not to site your heap in deep shade, where hungry tree roots will steal the plant foods and moisture. Evergreen hedges are also very greedy, so keep your heap away from them.

To increase aeration from below it is sensible to build your heap on brushwood. Some people go for wooden pallets or wire mesh, but if you create plenty of air channels through your heap you don't need to raise it off the ground, and composting can start quicker. Never build a compost heap on concrete or over plastic as this hampers aeration as well as keeping soil organisms away.

Compost bins holding materials in various stages of decomposition hidden behind an attractive willow-weave trellis.

Constructing cool heaps

First decide what size you want. You should aim for a heap at least 1 metre wide, deep, and tall. If it's any smaller it will have a hard time heating up at all and won't be able to retain warmth, so decomposition will be painfully slow, or may stop altogether. It will also dry out quickly and may even freeze in a cold winter.

However, an over-large heap can be difficult to manage, and unless you are very careful air won't be able to reach the centre and material will tend to pack down unevenly. If you need to aerate by hand it's hard work trying to turn a heap that's much taller or wider than 1.5 metres. If you have a lot of material to compost it's much better to make several smaller heaps than one huge one.

LAYERING MATERIALS

Always try and lay down as large a volume of material as possible to start a compost heap – even though it's fine to add materials gradually, as they're available, it's still best to add as much as you can in one go. It gives the organisms something to work with so they can get the whole process going, and so they don't starve.

A favourite composting formula is to start with a layer of branches and twigs, or build straight on the ground if you're confident of keeping the heap aerated. Then add a layer of grass mowings, or a layer of kitchen and garden waste that will rot down easily, followed by a dry layer of straw twigs or paper. Add a layer of muck and start again with grass. However, you are unlikely to often have materials in just this combination, so just try and layer your heap by alternating nitrogen-rich and fibre-rich layers, wetter with drier, and so on. You won't need much – or any – muck if you add plenty of other nitrogen-rich materials.

You can include layers of particular materials to make compost for specific conditions. Soil in most urban gardens is often slightly acid, so include a sprinkling of lime every few layers.

EASY COMPOST

The purpose of layering is to create a reasonably controlled mixture of different types of organic matter. But it is easier for a lot of home composters just to mix as you go, particularly if much of your compost is household waste. Keep the pieces of waste small or chop them, and add garden waste, or moist straw, or a touch of manure or topsoil every so often. If you grow your own produce and eat well you will produce varied nutrient-rich waste from kitchen and garden, and shouldn't need much else to make excellent compost. When your heap reaches the optimum size, cover it with a layer of earth and leave it for a few months before using it.

Composting grass mowings

The best place for grass mowings is on the grass, recycled into the lawn, where they break down slowly to release their nitrogen back to feed the grass. The next best place is on the compost heap. If you recycle yours, ask a non-composting neighbour for theirs.

There's a lot of nonsense talked about composting with grass clippings. They are nitrogen-rich and perfect for your compost heap. You shouldn't use thick layers of wet grass clippings, or of any other material, because they'll stop the rot by excluding air. As long as you are sensible and never add layers of more than 10–15 centimetres, grass clippings can be one of the most important nitrogen-providers in a compost pile, reducing the need to bring in muck from elsewhere, and usually freely available from March to September. It's not a good idea to use fresh grass mowings that have been recently treated with weedkiller or hormone-growth promoter straight away in a cool heap. Leave them to heat up and rot in a separate grass pile for two months, then you can add them to your compost, or use them as mulch, and they will still contain significant nitrogen.

Buried compost

One way of getting rid of your organic waste is to bury it in trenches. This is sometimes favoured by gardeners who dig the ground each year for planting vegetables, or before planting a permanent bed or feature, and is practical as long as you have reasonably light soil.

Dig a trench at least 30 centimetres deep (45centimetres minimum if you are going to plant a hedge) and fill it with organic materials. You don't need to be too fussy about proportions, but don't add very large chunks. Try to avoid very wet or completely dry matter, and don't throw in too thick a mass of bulky material – if there is too much fibre bacteria will have to work very hard to multiply rapidly and transform it into humus, and will steal vital nitrogen from the soil in the process. Mix everything well to try and ensure even decomposition, and top a trench with well-rotted manure or straw before backfilling with topsoil.

Don't practise trench composting in heavy clay soil or you are likely to end up with a smelly, slimy mass a few centimetres below the surface.

In hot countries pit composting is popular to keep moisture in and prevent heating from the sun. Compost heaps are built half underground and covered with soil or thick layers of leaves.

After backfilling a trench you'll end up with a slight surplus of topsoil. Put it to one side, covered, and use it in compost heaps or new beds.

Those windfall apples not suitable for juicing can be composted.

Strawy manure from pets or livestock makes wonderful composting material.

If in doubt, try to keep your heap three parts' vegetable matter to one part animal waste. If you don't want to use any animal products in your garden, substitute nitrogen-rich vegetable matter and extra minerals and compost activator for the animal matter.

Material should be packed loosely; make sure you chop or shred tougher bits and soak very dry stuff first.

Disadvantages

It's a useful way of disposing of most kitchen scraps and some garden waste, but trench composting scarcely generates heat, so weeds will flourish and anything with a shoot will probably grow – a handful of sprouting potato pieces will end up as a line of deep-rooted potatoes where you don't want them.

Don't grow root crops straight over a compost-filled trench for at least six months, by when the waste will have rotted, or crops may pick up unwanted bacteria. Some people suggest trench composting between the planting rows of a vegetable patch, moving the rows over each year, but you need to be extremely well organised and it would be better to make conventional compost to spread as mulch, or fork it in gently – it's not helpful to tread on your soil more than necessary; it harms the structure. Trench composting is generally better as a one-off system rather than an annual routine.

Hot heaps

If you want to make compost in a hurry you need to build a hot heap in one session. The best way to do this is to use a container because the composting conditions need to be as constant as possible.

Hot heaps work best if you use relatively even amounts of different materials, and there must be a variety of tough and tender materials. Include kitchen and household waste, grass clippings, weeds, and well-shredded prunings. Also have on hand some old straw or other bulky material, some manure and perhaps an additional compost activator. If you don't generate very much waste you will need to collect it all up for a couple of weeks in buckets and boxes or open-ended plastic sacks.

Mixing, layering, turning

Whether you choose to start with layers or mix everything together is largely a matter of personal preference. If you do layer, keep a balance and follow a soft layer with a more fibrous one, or nitrogen-rich material with carbon-rich (as for cool layering, page 65). Make sure there's a thin layer of soil every four or five layers, and include a compost activator. But a hot heap works just as well if everything is mixed before you start. Mix soft and stemmy materials, and make sure everything is slightly moist.

Fill the container to the edges and gently firm the contents down, so you don't leave any large gaps which could dry out. Cover the top with old carpet or polythene, and leave it for two weeks. Then turn the material. Dig or tip everything out of the container, re-mix it, moisten it if necessary, and return it to the bin with the material that was at the edges now at the centre. The more often you do this, the quicker you'll have finished compost, but if all is well you need only turn a heap once every two or three weeks to get finished compost in under three months.

Problem-solving

If you use a good variety of soft and tough materials, and watch temperature, air, and moisture, you should get excellent compost every time. Beginners to composting should turn their pile as often as possible, because it's a good way of checking what's happening.

Sometimes the compost may break down rather unevenly, with some materials decomposing very slowly. They may be too large, in which case remove them to go through another pile, or chop them further or split them by bashing with a hammer. Or you may have too much fibre for the amount of sappy material and you'll need to mix in more high-nitrogen material. Slightly rotted grass mowings or poultry manure are ideal.

If you get slimy patches, your heap may be too wet as well as airless – in which case aerobic bacteria can't survive to work. You may have included too much dense moist material such as grass mowings in one go, or without mixing them in properly. Remix everything well and add stemmy fibrous materials such as sunflower stems or moist straw in layers through the heap.

Dry patches also mean a problem with aeration and moisture. Check the pile of materials and water any that are too dry before putting them back in the bin, packed down evenly. Cover the container with plastic to keep moisture in. If one side of the compost seems to dry out faster than the other, your container is probably not sited in the best place, so you'll need to move it if practical, or insulate the more exposed side with straw bales.

Telltale smell

If your heap smells foul it is probably over-wet and under-aired. Turn it and add fibrous materials.

If it smells of ammonia it contains too much high-nitrogen material. Add fibre and turn it.

If the smell is sweet, the heap is damp but there's no heat. Add more nitrogen-rich material and turn it.

Which compost bin?

Don't be put off making a bin because your DIY skills are marginal. Sectional boxes can be built by even fairly incompetent carpenters. Cut twenty 17cm-long blocks of 5cm x 5cm timber and make five separate squares by nailing 15cm x 1m boards to the blocks, leaving a stump on either side. Place the first square on the ground and fill it, then add the next and so on. There will be a gap of approximately 2cm between each section for air to circulate. Fill all five square sections and use a square of carpet as a lid. It is easy to lift off the sections to turn the heap.

Once a cool composting system gets going well you should be able to remove compost from the bottom of a pile while adding raw materials at the top. A bin with solid sides and removable slats at the front can permit continuous supply.

The 'New Zealand Box' is a traditional 1.25m-square wooden compost box. Boards slot into the front between two posts so it is easy to add materials and remove compost. Some gardeners use them for hot composting and build them with slatted sides to allow extra aeration. You could build one from offcuts or reclaimed timber salvaged from skips, or haulage pallets. Three pallets wired together make an ideal compost box – just stick a couple of stakes in front to slot boards into.

If you have a large garden and plenty of materials to compost you can have two, or preferably three, adjoining boxes, or make one large box in two or three sections. Fill one section at a time and leave it to mature slowly while you fill the next one, using the most mature compost. Or if you're very keen, with lots of waste, you can use three bins for quantities of compost, moving the heaps between the bins.

Some tidy gardeners like to build permanent compost boxes out of bricks, breeze blocks, or even stone. If you do go for permanence, it's worth trying something else for a year, just to make sure you have chosen the best site, and never make a permanent concrete base.

INSULATION

They may not look neat, but straw bales make good compost surrounds, particularly in cool gardens, where they provide insulation. The optimum size heap uses thirteen bales, stacked three high on three sides with overlapping ends. You can pull more across to close up the front, and cover the heap with a sheet of carpet or corrugated iron. Re-use the straw in future batches of compost.

If you buy new timber to make a compost box, choose wood that has not been treated with chemical preservatives.

As long as you can keep it warm, moist, and aerated, and get at the finished compost, any container will do. Be inventive and make recycled compost containers from old plastic dustbins, discarded pallets or disused building materials.

Three-bin compost-fast

Make sure all materials are shredded, not too moist or dry, and watch the carbon/nitrogen ratio. You can get up to ten full bins of compost in one year using this method.

Week 1: Build a traditional layered hot heap in the centre bin, spread a layer of chopped leaves or straw in the adjoining holding bin and throw in kitchen and garden scraps daily.

Weeks 3, 4, 5: Turn the centre heap. Keep adding daily to the holding pile.

Week 6: Move the centre pile into the end bin. Move the holding pile into the centre bin, mixing all the materials well. Start a new pile in the original holding bin.

Weeks 7 and **8**: Turn the centre heap. Keep adding to the new holding pile. Turn the end heap.

Week 9: Check the compost in the end bin. It should be ready to use in the garden.

Continue the cycle for a permanent supply of compost. It will take longer in winter, and if your supply dries up or tapers off for a while, cover the maturing heaps with carpet or straw until things can speed up again.

Left, building your own boxes means you can have one or two composting while building the next one.

Any old iron?

Four sheets of corrugated iron, nailed to sturdy posts, make an excellent container. Drill a few lines of holes in the sides to encourage aeration, and stand on bare ground, then add garden and kitchen scraps as you have them.

CAGES AND METAL BINS

Stick four 1-metre-tall poles or stakes in the ground to make a 1-meter-diameter circle or square, wrap wire mesh round them, and you have a mesh compost bin.

These bins are great for leafmould and can make adequate compost bins if you insulate them well by wrapping carpet around the outside or cardboard inside, and cover the top with thick carpet. Their pluses are economy, ease of construction, and flexibility – join the mesh with wire clips and they can be dismantled in a trice, so you can turn your compost or move the bin to start a new compost pile in another part of the garden. The main minus is the need for insulation; and you need to watch aeration carefully.

An old metal dustbin can be transformed into a useful cool composting container. It is not large enough to make hot compost successfully unless you are prepared to turn the compost every few days, and even then success is not guaranteed. Drill holes in the sides, and a couple in the lid, for aeration, and site somewhere sheltered as the bin won't maintain heat effectively in cold weather. It is best if the bottom is pushed out so the bin stands straight onto soil and earthworms have easy access.

PLASTIC BINS AND TUMBLERS

There is a wide variety of plastic compost containers on the market. Always purchase the biggest container you can – it needs to be over 250 litres for effective composting. Anything smaller will have problems keeping heat in. For the same reason try to find a container with reasonably thick walls and a tight-fitting lid. If it has a base, make sure it has some holes for drainage, but it shouldn't need ventilation holes in the walls if you mix the right materials. You need to take just as much care in siting and feeding a compost container as any compost heap or pile.

Containers shaped like inverted cones work well because any condensed moisture trickles down the sides, allowing the centre to heat up well, without cooling, but keeping moisture in the pile. Square- and barrel-shaped containers are easy for access, for turning the compost, or for removing it.

TUMBLERS

Probably the most foolproof composting devices are compost tumblers; barrel shaped plastic containers mounted on an axle so you can turn the compost easily by tumbling the composter over. Daily turning means compost ingredients heat up well and keep well aerated for swift decomposition, so you can make finished compost in less than a month: fill the bin all at once if possible, mixing shredded ingredients together well, and when it is full turn it daily for two weeks. Then compost can be removed and the bin refilled. You can use this compost fresh on your garden, but it is best if it is left to mature under cover for a month or so.

The main advantages of tumblers are speed and good heating, so weed seeds and diseases are killed. Tumblers are self-contained so there is no risk of attracting vermin, and they can be used where there is no bare earth to site a heap or conventional bin. However, tumblers can be heavy to turn, and will not produce good compost unless they are turned regularly to ensure aeration.

Let worms eat your scraps

Worms compost waste by digesting it and converting the nutrients into a form plants can use. They excrete worm casts, which are rich in humus and a fine crumby texture, which is ideal for potting compost as well as an excellent soil-enricher. Worm pee is also an extremely powerful fertiliser.

Most compost systems require a bit of space, or effort, or both, plus a reasonable amount of waste. But worm composting requires only room for a box, takes little time or effort, and the worms only need kitchen scraps, which they recycle into very rich, crumbly compost and liquid fertiliser. Worm bins are ideal for small families with urban gardens, even balconies or roof gardens. Keen recyclers who only have houseplants and windowboxes can use them because worm bins can even be kept indoors – as long as a bin is working properly it won't give off any offensive smells or attract bugs.

WORMS' NEEDS

Like conventional compost systems, worm bins need warmth, air and moisture. Worms have to have moist skin in order to breathe – they need air so the material doesn't get waterlogged and smelly, and they are most productive between 18 and 28°C, so a bin needs to be well insulated if it lives outside in winter, and shaded in summer. The best times to start a worm bin are spring and summer, when temperatures are ideal and worms are hungriest. Provide your worms with moist, crumbly bedding and keep them in the dark. They also need a slightly alkaline environment, so keep an eye on their diet.

Unlike other compost systems, worms need feeding little and often, not much bulk – they are much more likely to die from overfeeding than from starvation. Worms will eat almost anything as long as it is chopped small, but concentrate on kitchen scraps – they won't destroy perennial weeds, weed seeds or diseased plant material.

Worm bins

Like other compost containers, a worm bin should keep moisture in and rain out, allow some air to circulate, and be able to maintain a fairly constant temperature. You can buy a custom-built plastic bin or wooden box complete with worms, but it is more economical and not difficult to recycle an old box or large drawer, or convert a plastic dustbin. Brandling or tiger worms are freely available in muck heaps or from fishing tackle shops.

Kitchen scraps are ideal worm bin fodder. The worms feed on the soft bits as they rot rather than chewing up the entire scraps. As they consume rotting material as it appears there should be no smell of rotten waste.

As long as your worm bin and the container where you collect the food scraps are well covered there should never be a problem with flies.

The more worms you have, the quicker the composting, but it is best to start with a small colony of about a hundred worms until you know you've got the conditions right.

Worms die in acid conditions. Their ideal pH is around 7. Don't feed them too much acid food, and add a sprinkling of ground lime with their food every few weeks.

A worm bin doesn't need to be very tall, but choose a wide container rather than a narrow one as worms feed near the surface so the greater the surface area the more compost they'll produce.

Wooden or plastic

An ideal size wooden box is around 60 centimetres square and 30 tall. Never use chemically treated wood. Simply drill some holes in the base for drainage and line the box with a single layer of pebbles before adding worm bedding. Find or make a lid, which should have cracks for air. If you convert a dustbin drill two lines of drainage holes about 10 and 15centimetres from the base, and make ventilation holes in the lid, which should fit tightly for insulation and to stop flies. To keep humidity fill the bottom 10 centimetres with pebbles and sand, and add water until it seeps from the drainage holes. Put the bedding on top of the pebbles – you may want to lay gauze first, so the bedding and compost remains slightly separate from the stones.

There won't be much seepage from a wooden box, so a newspaper underneath the box should be sufficient to stop puddles. But plastic bins will leak. Commercial bins are often fitted with a tap for siphoning off the liquid, which can be diluted 10:1 and used as liquid feed. Place a tray under a home-made bin and either drain it regularly to catch the more dilute liquid, or place a layer of compost on it and change it every two or three weeks, using the moistened compost on houseplants or in the garden.

Getting going

Mix up a bucketful of well-rotted compost, muck, or leafmould (but not made from beech or oak leaves as this tends to be acidic) with some shredded newspaper. Moisten the mixture thoroughly, then lay this bedding about 10 centimetres deep over the pebbles, and your worm home is ready for occupation. You'll need at least one hundred worms to start your colony. If you collect them from a compost heap bring a little of this material with them, otherwise just lay your worms in the centre of the bedding, and cover them with a couple of layers of moist newspaper.

Worms will eat any kitchen scraps, but don't give them too much citrus fruit or acid food. Chop scraps finely – some people liquidise them, but this isn't strictly necessary. Worms can eat any cooked remains, including meat and fish scraps, but can't eat very dry food.

If you look in a pile of rotting manure or maturing compost you'll see dozens of small red worms with yellow bands. These are brandling or tiger worms (Eisenia foetida). They are the worms traditionally used as fishing bait and in composting systems.

Worms don't like too much food at once, so start with no more than 1 litre or 500 grams of finely shredded food spread on top of the bedding around 5 centimetres deep. Don't cover the whole surface. You can partially bury food, but then it's hard to tell when to add more, and worms are not deep-feeders, so some buried scraps may not get processed. Wait until the previous offerings have been well integrated before adding more. Keep the food moist and always cover it with moistened newspaper.

EXTRACTING COMPOST

You can remove compost a little at a time whenever you want, but if you want to wait for a binful – the speed depends how much food is added, how many worms you have, and the temperature – empty it in spring or summer so you can get your colony going again quickly. Remove the worms in a small amount of compost and leave them on one side, covered with moist newspaper, empty the bin, and put the worms back in to start again. If you have masses of worms, start two colonies.

Keeping healthy

If your bin starts to smell it means the worms aren't processing the food quickly enough. Reduce feeding – make a second bin if you have too many scraps – and check the moisture, temperature, and pH of the compost.

If the contents of the bin get soggy, check the drainage holes aren't blocked. Mix in shredded newspaper or coir to soak up excess moisture, and don't add extra liquid to the worm food.

Sometimes worms gather around the lid of the bin. If there are just a few this is nothing to worry about, but if they all seem to be trying to escape check pH, moisture, ventilation, and temperature, and be careful about feeding. You can remove the worms, with a little compost, and cover them with moistened newspaper while you clear out the bin and start again.

time and space

*good gardening is knowing
when and where to act*

time and space

After building soil fertility, planning your planting is the next most important step to successful organic gardening.

It's not hard to find suppliers of organic seeds, but if you have problems, have a go with whatever is available at your supermarket; the end results will still be delicious and healthy . Bear in mind, though, that mass-marketed seeds are not organic and are therefore grown in conditions with chemical support. They are often coated in a protective fungicidal material. However, in your organic garden these seeds will have to look after themselves without chemical support and this may not be as easy as starting off with organic seeds.

Seeds – sources and saving

Organic seeds are now widely available. Although they are often more expensive as they are not produced on such a large scale, they are still good value when you consider what you get from them. To overcome this many organic gardeners organise seed-swapping groups.

VARIETY AND VARIATION

It is important to select the right variety of plant for your requirements. Within each species there are varieties adapted to certain conditions. There are, for example, over five hundred varieties of potato. Each one is best suited to certain conditions, with its own particular strengths and weaknesses when it comes to pest and disease resistance, and each with its own growing requirements.

Within each variety there is still genetic variation. Unless plants are taken from asexual reproduction such as cuttings or runners, each plant will be slightly different from another. This is the basis upon which evolution works. Without individual variety there would be nothing for natural selection to work on. One of the important tenets of organic gardening is to plant the most appropriate variety of a plant for your particular garden. Better still, the best variety for the particular spot within your garden. This is working with nature rather than against it.

BIODIVERSITY

Another important rule of organic gardening is to maximise biodiversity (different types of plants and animals) in the garden. This means maximising genetic variety by planting more than one variety of each species. But it also means planting a rich variety of different species of plants. These different species and varieties will attract a wider range of wildlife than a less diverse flora. This means that the overall biodiversity of your garden is increased and this improves the likelihood of ecological balance.

Left, some of the many different varieties of edible bean.

High biodiversity helps us all by keeping our options open for the future. The more genetic diversity we have to draw upon, the more potential there is for adapting to changing conditions in the future.

SPECIAL SEEDS

As organic gardeners we aim to protect the health and welfare of other people and wildlife, so we are interested in protecting endangered species and varieties of plants for future generations. The seeds that are marketed today are those selected for promotion by the major seed companies. If a variety is not on that list, it is not grown for seed, promoted, or distributed and, as a result, many varieties are in danger of dying out. In recent decades, seed companies have concentrated their efforts on genetically engineered hybrids, which are more profitable. Not only can hybrid varieties produce attractive qualities such as higher yields or faster growth, the customer also has to buy new seed from the seed company each year.

Old traditional plants are open-pollinated and produce viable seeds, but fewer and fewer are offered through mainstream catalogues today. These old varieties are often best suited to organic gardening, and you may be able to find specific varieties suited to your region and your requirements.

One of the aims of the organic gardeners' associations such as Henry Doubleday Research Association (HDRA) is to catalogue known varieties and co-ordinate seed-saving between growers. A successful example of this has been the recovery of the rare but beautiful purple flowering broad bean. You could get involved in growing and protecting historical or local varieties adapted to your region.

Growing for your garden

Those plants that do well in your garden are obviously enjoying the conditions you provide, so it is sensible to save their seeds to replant next year. Those plants that are struggling and battling with disease or pests in your garden are best left to the compost heap.

HOW TO SAVE YOUR OWN SEEDS

If you want to save your own seed from a plant, make sure that the original seed was not an F1 hybrid. To be sure of what you will get try to ensure that the plants did not cross-pollinate with other varieties. Select the plants that did best in your garden and have the characteristics you prefer, and leave a few to go to seed. For those

Dwarf beans left to mature for seed-saving.

Most seeds remain viable for many years, but some, like carrots and parsnips, only really last until the next spring.

Many seeds marketed today are F1 hybrids, meaning that they are sterile and you will be unable to save your own seed from them.

Do not use plastic bags to store seeds as they will rot unless completely dry. Sealed paper envelopes are an effective way to store your collected seeds. Don't forget to label and date them.

Coriander plants drying out in the greenhouse. Seeds are used for re-sowing and cooking.

As some perennials take a long time to mature, use the space around and beneath them while they are young to grow shorter-lived perennial plants. While apple trees are getting established, for example, you can get years of production from currant bushes in between before the tree canopies shade them out too much.

plants that produce seed heads containing many tiny seeds, such as poppies, wait until they are dry but have not yet shed their seeds, carefully cut the stems and hang them upside down into a paper bag. For plants that produce bigger seeds, such as beans, simply pick the pods when they are thoroughly dry, remove the beans and store in paper envelopes to finish drying before storing in airtight jars.

Some seeds need to be carefully prepared for drying. The most important thing is to get rid of excess water. Seeds of tomatoes and squash, for example, need to be extracted from the moist pulp that surrounds them, rinsed, and dried on paper towels in a dark, well-ventilated area. When they are dry, they can be placed in paper envelopes to finish drying before being stored in an airtight jars.

Sowing and planting

Plan your sowing and planting through the year in order to make best use of your garden. Once you know what you want to grow and where it should go, you will need to work out when each plant will reach its best (flower or ripen). This way you can make sure you get as much colour, interest, and food as is possible all year round. You can extend the season of colour and food by using protective structures (see page 98), selecting a range of varieties, and sowing and planting at regular intervals through the year.

GIVING SEEDS A HEAD START

Fork compost into a seed bed three or four weeks before sowing seeds. Be sure it is well rotted, as unfinished compost can sometimes retard seed germination. Some gardeners never dig their soil. Instead, they prefer to add 5–10-centimetre layers of compost annually or bi-annually. All sowing and planting takes place through the compost.

When you prepare a seed bed for your cultivated vegetables and annual flowers, you are also creating perfect conditions for many weed seeds. You can sow your chosen seed very thickly, to compete aggressively with weed seeds, thinning out your plants later. But a better way is to cheat weeds into getting going before your chosen seeds. This is ideal in soils that warm up early in spring.

The trick is to prepare your seed bed two weeks earlier than you want to plant your first seeds. Cover it with clear plastic or horticultural fleece, to warm the ground. A first flush of annual weeds will take advantage of the conditions, and will quickly germinate and sprout. Leave this so-called 'stale seed bed' for two weeks, when most seeds will have sprouted. Then, hoe them off, leave their decaying remains as a nitrogen-rich mulch, and sow your seeds as usual. This technique won't get rid of all your weeds, but it will remove most competition from your chosen plants when they are most vulnerable.

The best way to reduce weed competition in heavier soils is to sow seeds into modules or small containers. Then, plant them out when they are strong enough to outgrow any weeds, and when you have had the chance to hoe or pull out early starters. It is also much easier to remove weeds around recognisable seedlings than around small sprouts.

SELF-SOWING AND DIRECT SOWING

Self-seeders, such as poppies and nasturtiums, will reproduce themselves in your garden without human interference. You can easily pull up unwanted seedlings should they stray too far from your desired locations. Many vegetables are best sown directly outside as they dislike the shock of transplantation. Different seeds need different conditions for germination and you will need to read the instructions on the seed packet carefully. Generally, though, direct sowing is never one hundred per cent successful, so sow more densely than you require, to allow for failures. You can thin out surplus seedlings later, when you are confident that they are healthy.

INDOORS TO OUTDOORS

Although some plants are suitable for sowing directly into the ground, most will benefit from getting off to a good start indoors or in a cold frame. By sowing into modules seedlings will have less of a transplanting shock to deal with late – especially if the modules are biodegradable. As with direct sowing, sow a few more than you want to end up with. You might sow three carrot seeds in each module and later plant them out as a complete bunch. This is a good technique to produce 'baby' vegetables. Or you might thin the seedlings to one carrot per module at an early stage, before planting out. Module-sown seedlings have less difficulty competing with weeds than direct-sown.

Before planting seedlings outside, you will need to harden them off. This means gradually acclimatising them to the harsher conditions. Start by putting them outside during the day for a few weeks, until they have clearly become hardened to the conditions.

Wherever possible, sow seeds into 'plugs' or 'modules' that decompose, so you can place the pot straight into the soil. Recycle cardboard egg boxes, use tubes of newspaper twisted at the base, or buy compressed coir or paper pots.

As a general rule, seeds should be sown to a depth equal to their length, e.g. broad beans of 1cm length are sown 1cm deep. Carrot seeds of 3mm length are barely covered with a sprinkling of soil.

Common problems with sowing:

Damping off is a fungal disease that comes with excessive watering or fertilising, a lack of sun, or poor air circulation.

Avoid by watering indoor trays from below and improving air circulation.

Leggy seedlings are pale-stemmed, tall, and weak. They are caused by poor light.

Avoid by providing adequate light and brushing your hand gently over seedlings to encourage thickening of stems.

ROWS OR GRIDS

Decide in advance how you are going to arrange the plants. In the vegetable plot traditional straight lines may be easy to harvest, but can leave areas of bare ground. Hexagonal grid patterns make more efficient use of space. Sow or plant one at each corner of the grid and one in the middle. In this pattern, mature plants create a canopy that covers all the bare ground. This reduces moisture loss and the opportunity for weeds to compete.

SUCCESSION

For crops that don't keep well, plan a succession of sowings throughout the season. For a continuous supply of fresh lettuces, spinach, peas, radishes, and calabrese, you might sow a small batch every two to four weeks. Don't forget to leave room for successive sowings in your planting plan.

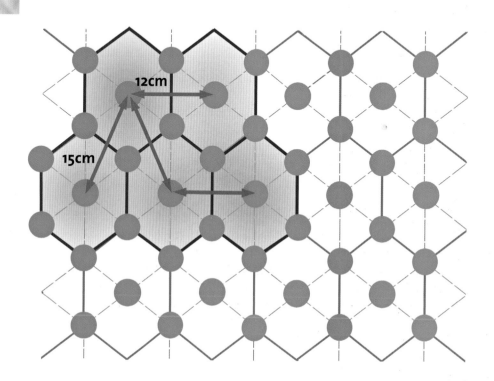

Hexagonal planting schemes space plants closer together than in rows. For example, if plants can be sown or planted in rows 15cm apart, they can go 12cm apart in a hexagonal pattern.

Edible Landscapes

You may want organic food crops, but also want beautiful ornamentals in a small space. Don't worry. You can have both. Create an edible landscape by planting edible, decorative plants (including flowers) and attractive food crops. Many fruit trees have beautiful blossoms and foliage. Instead of planting a dogwood just as an ornamental, try planting a variety such as *Cornus Kousa* or *Cornus Mas,* which produce edible berries as well. Similarly, there are varieties of honeysuckle that produce edible berries.

Left, cottage garden with herbs, flower, and vegetables all interplanted.

Right, edible nasturtiums interplanted with attractive varieties of lettuce.

GET MORE FOR LESS

Take advantage of the way plants grow at different rates to sow fast-growing ones around slower ones. That way you can use the same space for two crops or more in one season, and keep the ground constantly covered so weeds can't get a foothold. Sow radishes, for example, in spring, between other salads. Sow fast-growing leafy lettuces around slender-leaved, slow-growing garlic and onions. Use fast-growing brassicas, such as rocket and mustards, around peas and beans.

Intercropping is a great way to increase diversity and make best use of the limited space available in the garden. Some plants, like sweetcorn, are destined to be big, needing wide spacing, but take a while to grow. You can interplant a crop underneath, such as low-spreading squash, which tolerates the light shade and successfully covers the bare ground.

Another way to get more for less is to use multi-functional plants, which provide ornamental, edible, and medicinal payoffs.

Sweetcorn underplanted with squash.

Multifunctional plants

Some plants are particularly useful in a small garden because they serve more than one purpose. The elder shrub (*Sambucus spp.*) is one such plant.

Ornamental (available in green, gold, and purple). Keep it cut well back for abundant fresh colour each year.

Large, ornate, edible flower heads in spring. High in potassium.

Ornate edible berries in autumn. High in vitamin C.

Elder's hollow stems have many potential uses. In the past they were used for making musical pipes or as a means of blowing flames on open fires.

Flowers can be used to make a cordial or brewed to make an alcoholic 'champagne'.

Berries can be brewed to make wine.

The flowers and berries are medicinal used by herbalists to clear fever, phlegm, cold and flu symptoms by promoting sweating, urination, and reducing inflammation.

The leaves and stems are only recommended for external use as a fly-repellant and insecticide for livestock.

Crop rotation

Try to avoid growing the same vegetables in the same positions in your garden year after year, as this can lead to problems with soil pests, diseases, and fertility.

Crop rotation should be followed as far as possible, even in a small garden. The standard technique is to use a four-year rotation to avoid the build up of crop-specific soil pests and diseases. For example, onion white rot will build up to attack onions, garlic, and leeks; eelworms attack peas, beans, onions, and potatoes; and clubroot can harm all brassicas. By rotating these crops you help avoid prolonging disease problems.

Some people say that rotation makes little difference to pest and disease control in a small garden, but at the very least, it is still a valuable way of improving your soil.

Different crops take different things from the soil, so if you grow one species continually this can exhaust the soil of a particular range of nutrients. But if you change crops each year you replenish the soil with different elements. For example, legumes (peas and beans) are useful in a crop rotation system because they provide the soil with nitrogen to feed a following crop. Rotation also helps your soil structure, particularly when you grow a range of shallow-rooting and deep-rooting plants. Rotation also helps control weeds. Greedy feeders and bushy plants such as potatoes and squash, for example, are good at clearing ground for a following crop.

VEGETABLE ROTATION SYSTEMS

A traditional system rotates potatoes, brassicas, legumes, and roots on a four-year cycle, but few home gardeners follow this slavishly. First of all think, about what you want to grow and eat. There's no point in growing something you don't want just because it fits into a fertility system. Then think about the different needs of specific plants. For example, leafy greens and brassicas thrive in soil where beans have fixed plenty of nitrogen; onions like well-fed soil, but carrots and parsnips will 'fork' in too-rich conditions; potatoes don't like lime.

Try to leave room for regular green manure crops for cover and structure, and remember to fit them into the rotation system. Don't follow cabbages with mustard, for example, as they are both brassicas. Try to get into the habit of planning carefully, and keep good records of what you plant and when you harvest. But you'll learn most by your successes, and by any failures.

General rules for planning your own rotation

Never follow this year's crop with another from the same family (see list of botanical families).

Roots take a lot out of the soil, so put them before legumes.

Brassicas love limed soil.

Green manure in rotation.

Muck before potatoes, but don't muck before root crops.

Greens that require regular watering are best kept together and away from root crops that need less water.

Botanical families
Brassicas
Brussels sprouts, cabbages, cauliflowers, kale, radishes, swedes, turnips, mustard.
Legumes
Peas, beans, alfalfa, clover, vetches, lucerne.
Potato family
Potatoes, tomatoes, aubergines, peppers.
Umbellifers
Carrots, parsnips, celery, parsley, fennel.
Daisy family
Lettuce, chicory, endive, scorzonera.
Onion family
Onions, garlic, leeks, chives.
Beetroot family
Beetroot, spinach, chard.
Cucurbit family
Courgettes, marrows, squash, cucumbers.

spring/summer

ARLY AND MAIN CROP POTATOES, TOMATOES
*apply manure in spring
before planting potatoes*

plot a

LEGUMES
(*and onions/leeks/garlic
from previous year*)

CARROTS, BEETROOT, PARSNIP

plot d

BRASSICAS
*apply compost in
spring and summer*

plot b

plot c

*This is one example of a
basic four-year rotation
plan suitable for the UK, as
recommended by HDRA.
Crops and soil treatments
move round the beds anti-
clockwise. Some crops will
overlap as new crops catch
up with longer-term ones.*

autumn/winter

plot a

AUTUMN-PLANTED ONIONS

WINTER TARES
*apply lime if needed
(see page 26)*

plot d

PHACELIA OR GRAZING RYE

WINTER CABBAGE
apply leafmould

plot b

plot c

The crops left out of your rotation are either the permanent crops that must not be disturbed, or plants like Jerusalem artichokes that grow very tall and so need growing at one end of the garden. Annual herbs like parsley and chives make excellent edgings. Catch crops, like radish and lettuce, can be grown almost anywhere, fitting in as they do where convenient.

IGNORING ROTATION

Sometimes it may not be practical to follow a rotation system – for example, only one part of your garden may be sunny or warm enough for certain crops, or in a very small garden you may want to concentrate on quick-growing vegetables or summer salads. As long as you maintain your soil in good condition, keep adding plenty of organic matter and don't grow exactly the same thing in the same place two years running, then you should safely be able to grow most things without too much worry. Just keep an eye out for any problems and never follow an infested or diseased crop with the same species.

Using rotation, intercropping, and successive sowings, you will need to keep accurate records of what you did and what happened each year. This way you will soon build up a system that works for you in your particular garden.

If bed space is limited, ease difficulties with rotation and grow some vegetables in containers.

Leafy salad vegetables and other swift-growing, shallow-rooted vegetables can be grown between other crops.

Never grow tomatoes in the same place where potatoes have grown the previous year, as they are members of the same family.

Tomatoes and courgettes grow happily in compost-filled tyres.

Why legumes are useful

Most plants cannot take in nitrogen from the air, yet they need it to grow. Soil bacteria can fix some nitrogen, but by far the greatest quantity is fixed by leguminous plants.

Legumes play a useful role in making nitrogen available to other plants. They have specialised nodules on their roots which house nitrogen-fixing bacteria commonly of the Rhizobium species. These bacteria take nitrogen from the soil air and convert it into ammonia, which the plant can use to make proteins. In return, the bacteria get food from the plants.

When the leguminous plant is cut back or dug into the soil, decomposition releases the fixed nitrogen in a form other plants can use.

Background image, root nodules containing nitrogen-fixing bacteria.

Perennial vegetables

When we think of growing organic vegetables we usually think of annual or biennial crops that come and go in our vegetable plot. But there are a range of perennial vegetables which are low-maintenance and provide food at times when there is little else coming from the garden.

Perennials form the backbone of permaculture – a system of growing food and other resources that maximises the use of permanent plantings and efficiently integrates all the elements of a particular site. The result is a low-maintenance, high-diversity plot. Permaculture designs often include a forest garden packed with perennial vegetables, herbs, and fruits in vertical layers, from ground cover to tree tops. As suitable plant varieties have experienced less artificial selection for yield than annual vegetables, they can be less productive per plant. However, because of the high diversity, stacking and interplanting, overall yield per area can be good.

Those perennial vegetables most common in the UK include: asparagus and artichoke (globe and Jerusalem). However, specialist research team 'Plants for a Future' list over five thousand perennial food plants that will grow outside in the UK. Just a few are listed here:

Some of the plants we treat as annuals in the vegetable garden are in fact perennial under the right conditions. Peppers, for example, are perennial in a frost-free environment.

Sweet potato (Ipomea batters) can be grown as the perennial if it is in a frost-free greenhouse or polytunnel.

Seeds

Araucaria araucana (Monkey puzzle)
Caragana arborescens (Siberian pea tree)
Castanea sativa (Sweet chestnut)
Cephalotaxus drupacea harringtonii Corylus species
    (Cobnuts and Filberts)
Juglans regia (Walnut)
Quercus ilex (Holm oak)

All bear well at least in parts of Britain.

Roots

Erythronium species (Dog's tooth violets)
Lathyrus tuberosus; *Lilium lancifolium* (Tiger lily)
Medeola virginica (Cucumber root) and *Streptopus
    amplexifolius* .

Leaves

Allium ursinum (Wild garlic)
Campanula persicifolia (Harebell)
Cryptotaenia japonica (Japanese parsley)
Fagopyrum dibotrys (Perennial buckwheat)
Montia sibirica (Miner's lettuce)
Myrrhis odorata (Sweet Cicely)
Rumex acetosa (Sorrel)
Tilia species (Lime trees)
Urtica dioica (Stinging nettles)
Viola odorata (Sweet violet)

Theses are just a few of the species to choose from and between them you should be able to pick fresh leaves all the year round.

Fruits

Take your choice of fruit trees and shrubs, but don't limit yourself to apples, pears, raspberries, and blackcurrants. Check out the exciting possibilities of hardy juneberries, grapes, almonds, peaches, and kiwi fruits. For tips on planting fruit trees, see page 104.

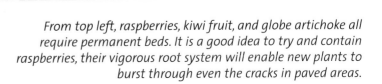

Perennial food crops

Trees, shrubs, and perennial herbs need to be planted in permanent planting areas, but there are other fruits and vegetables which require permanent beds, too. Rhubarb, strawberries, and globe artichokes need to planted into well-prepared soil, mulched and top-dressed each year with compost.

From top left, raspberries, kiwi fruit, and globe artichoke all require permanent beds. It is a good idea to try and contain raspberries, their vigorous root system will enable new plants to burst through even the cracks in paved areas.

Beds and strips

The key to successful gardening is never to take on too much at one go. A sensible first step, particularly for vegetable growers, is to divide your plot into manageable beds, separated by paths. No-dig gardeners usually use beds, and it is an equally useful soil management strategy for conventional dig-and-mulch gardeners, even if you have a large garden with a substantial area dedicated to fruit and vegetables.

Growing in beds means you can concentrate your resources on the areas that need them. It is much more productive, for example, to spread organic matter thickly over a dedicated area, rather than a blanket approach. The fertility of a few, small areas can be built up quickly compared to tackling a large area.

IDEAL BEDS

The best width for beds is around 1.5 metres, so that you can reach the centre of a bed without ever treading on the soil. Paths should be wide enough to take a wheelbarrow. All weeding, cultivating, and planting should be done from the paths so you will never compact the soil and harm the structure by treading on it.

Even difficult soil in beds can be worked at most times of the year because there is no fear of compaction when cultivating. You can also plant closer together in beds than in more open ground, which means you have fewer weed problems, but grow more produce. If you make a minimum of four beds, however small, this makes rotation simple to manage, further helping to maintain your soil health and fertility.

Avoid edging beds with wood which has been preserved using toxic chemicals.

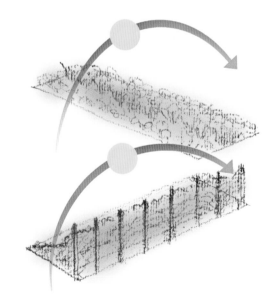

If your beds are oval or rectangular, lay them north–south so that you can plant taller plants at the north side to minimise their shading effect.

RAISED BEDS

You can grow plants more closely together in deep, raised beds than in ground-level planting because of the depth of organic matter. You will never need to dig, and soil structure and fertility should maintain themselves with nothing more than regular addition of compost.

MAKING RAISED BEDS

Beds can be as high as you find comfortable. For best results, double dig the area first, or at least aerate the subsoil thoroughly with a fork. Make sure your raised beds are no more than two arms' reach in breadth for ease of working, and mark them out with an edging of your choice. Wooden boards are practical, but avoid those treated with chemicals, or use bricks, tiles, stones, depending on what is available locally. You will then need to fill the bed to the required depth with a mixture of topsoil, compost, and other organic matter.

Unless you are using loam made from your own turf-stacks, watch out for the quality of imported topsoil – it can be very sterile and full of weed seeds. Ideally, make raised beds in autumn and sheet mulch with cardboard covered with a layer of organic matter through which you can plant in spring. If you need to make higher raised beds, make sure the edging is sturdy enough to take the large volume of soil and compost.

Edging raised beds
1) sharpened logs 2). sharpened split logs 3) planks of wood held in place with short posts 4) split logs make a natural edging 5) reused bricks can be used to make taller raised beds 6) local stone also makes an attractive permanent barrier to raised beds.

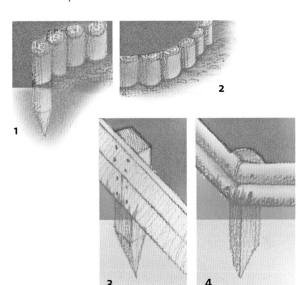

1

2

3

4

5

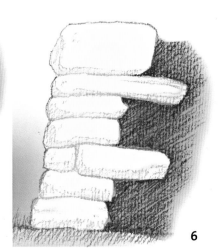

6

Growing in containers

Where space is limited, many plants can be grown successfully in containers, but sometimes even the most experienced gardeners have difficulty growing in pots. Just as in the garden, the secret is the soil. It should be light and loose for drainage and air, but not so light that nutrients drain straight away. While soil structure and fertility in the garden is maintained via all the living creatures and micro-organisms, you can't create a living soil in a container, so you have to follow different rules.

Garden soil is a poor growing medium for plants in containers. Soil compacts much more easily in a pot than in the garden, quickly becoming heavy and airless. Every time you water the soil tends to settle, and there are no living organisms to stir it up again. Container soil therefore needs to be much looser than garden soil. You can use a proprietary potting compost, or make your own from loam, well-rotted composts and sand or grit – then you know exactly what's in it.

The best soil base for potting compost is loam from turf stacks, or molehills where soil is weed-free and well broken down into crumbs. If you use garden soil as a base, sterilise it first to kill any disease organisms and weed seeds by baking it at around 180°C in the oven for 30 minutes.

CONTAINER SIZE

Avoid stress on container-grown plants by making sure their pots are the right size for them. A plant will tell you when it needs repotting by wilting easily and sending roots out through the container's drainage holes. Always repot into a container that is only one size larger than the one your plant has grown out of. Soil in a big pot containing a small plant will always stay wet so the plant runs the risk of root rot and other stress.

Vegetables suitable for growing in containers include:

asparagus pea	courgette
aubergine	lettuce
broad bean	spring onion
French bean	tomato (dwarf and bush types)
beetroot	spinach
carrot	swiss chard
corn salad	any of the cut-and-come-again crops

Container soil should have a loose, crumbly texture to absorb nutrients, but retain air and drain easily. It must contain plenty of food supplies. Use a mixture of garden loam or molehill soil and well-rotted leafmould for the base, adding blood, fishmeal, bonemeal, worm compost or well-rotted garden compost for nutrients, and sand or grit for extra aeration.

Garden compost is a fertiliser and soil conditioner, and can't be used on its own as potting compost. Worm compost, however, makes ideal potting compost.

Garden soil should only be used as a base for permanent plantings in large containers, such as fruit trees or large shrubs.

Foliar-feed your container-grown plants with liquid fertilisers (see page 106).

Container-grown plants can be moved around the garden to make best use of space as different times of year. Above, container-grown herbs get an extra boost of summer sun in a crowded garden.

Growing under cover

The space in your garden can be made even more useful by incorporating some structures that protect plants from damaging weather, pesky herbivores, or unwanted cross-pollination. Protective structures create a warmer microclimate that increases the rate of photosynthesis (as long as there is sufficient light and water), which means they can improve yields, speed of growth, and extend the growing season.

Cloches

Simple, portable transparent covers made of glass or plastic. They can be placed over seedlings while they get established or over tender plants when frost threatens. Some are beautifully ornate structures, such as the traditional Victorian glass frames. Other modern-day reused structures, such as cut-off, clear plastic bottles, are less attractive, but create a suitable microclimate even so.

Cold frames

These are more permanent or semi-portable structures with opening vents. You can make a simple cold frame using straw bales and old windows. Cold frames provide additional heat, protection from frost and wind damage. If you sow seeds indoors, you will need to harden them off in a cold frame before planting them outside.

Hot beds

A variant of the cold frame is the heated frame or hot bed. Traditionally, frames were placed on top of rotting manure, which gave off heat as it decomposed. Nowadays, most hot frames are heated with an electric heating cable. Hot beds can be used to grow some unusual plants – especially if the hot bed is made inside a greenhouse or polytunnel. Even in the UK, pineapples can fruit growing in a hot bed of decomposing horse muck.

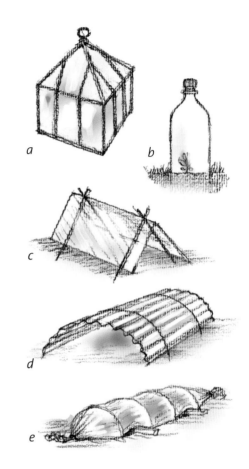

Different cloche styles: a) glass lantern, b) cut-off plastic bottle, c) traditional glass tent, d) rigid plastic tunnel, e) polythene over hoops.

Manure heaped around sides to add heat.

Firmly trodden manure in a pit under the frame.

Fleeces

A simple protection against moderate frost is horticultural fleece – a light, transparent fabric that acts like a temporary greenhouse, trapping heat and protecting against wind and herbivore damage. To avoid damage from fleece rubbing on plants, put a few sticks or canes underneath and protect the sharp tips with recycled yoghurt pots. Or, lay the fleece over plastic hoops made of reused waterpipe (see right). Make sure the edges are securely pinned down or buried into the soil.

Right, carrots under fleece supported by plastic hoops protects them from carrot fly (see page 148).

When using protective structures, make sure you are not covering up a plant that needs to be pollinated by wind or insect-borne pollen.

GREENHOUSE OR POLYTUNNEL

An unheated greenhouse gets warm because glass allows sunlight in, but does not so readily let heat out again. For this to work, obviously the greenhouse needs to be cited in sunlight – the south side of the house in the northern hemisphere and the north side in the southern hemisphere. Make sure ventilation is available and checked regularly. And, of course, being under glass you will need to water the plants systematically.

Heating a greenhouse is not necessarily economical. However, a heated greenhouse will give you a completely different set of conditions that allow you to grow crops from different climates and to keep plants frost-free all year. You can focus the heat under seedling beds with electrical cable or build a hot bed in the greenhouse. For warmth at no extra cost, you can store rain water run-off in large black containers housed inside. These large black objects act as heat reservoirs, slowly releasing the day's heat at night.

Polytunnels are walk-in structures made of large hoops, covered in polythene buried into the soil on either side. The cover needs replacing about every four years and tears can easily be mended with specialized tape. Polytunnels are not frost-free all year, so beware. Again think about ventilation as they can get very hot in summer, but on the plus side, they do allow wind or insect pollination. For maximum sunlight place the longest axis of the tunnel east–west in the northern hemisphere.

A greenhouse or a polytunnel is a great bonus to an organic garden. They:

* ❀ *Extend the length of the growing season*
* ❀ *Allow you to grow crops that you could not otherwise grow in this country*
* ❀ *Improve growing conditions, e.g. tomatoes ripen better indoors*
* ❀ *Provide a winter-growing season for frost-tolerant crops*
* ❀ *Isolate rare species such as heritage plants from cross-pollination*

Indoor winter crops
(sow in autumn in the unheated polytunnel or greenhouse):

carrot

chicory

Chinese greens

endive

lamb's lettuce *(as cut-and-come-again all winter)*

lettuce *(autumn and winter varieties)*

radish *(winter variety)*

parsley

peas *(winter hardy variety)*

perpetual spinach

Left, lean-to greenhouse containing annual and perennial food crops, herbs, and drying space. As a bonus, the lean-to also warms the home.

Above, polytunnels offer a range of different possibilities to the traditional greenhouse.

As permanent, protective structures, the greenhouse or polytunnel will need at least a water supply and possibly electricity for heating and lighting. Garden soil is not ideal for indoor beds. Compost is best. Maintain soil health by top-dressing with compost each spring and autumn, and adhere to crop rotation inside, just as you would outside.

As with the rest of your garden, try to maintain biodiversity inside and keep a watchful eye for diseased plants, so that they can be rapidly removed.

Above, a nectarine is underplanted with carrot. Left, fig, peach, and tomato on an unheated greenhouse wall with (right) basil, tagetes, and parsley underplanted.

Planting perennials

Careful planning should ensure that your perennial trees, shrubs, herbs, ornamentals, and vegetables go where the soil and microclimate best suit their needs. Plums, for example, can thrive on clay soils, while apples prefer a lighter soil (see page 27).

When planting perennials make the hole bigger than the root area, dig the base of the hole to improve drainage and incorporate plenty of well-rotted manure or compost. Loosen all the soil around the sides of the hole, too. Plant the perennial to the depth of the soil mark on the stem. With bare-rooted plants, spread the roots out. With container-grown plants carefully tease out a few leading roots so that they can grow away from the root ball. Sprinkle well-conditioned soil over the roots and water well.

Insert your stakes at this stage so you can avoid damaging the roots. Then backfill with soil and compost, shaking the plant gently to allow the soil to settle in between the roots. Finally, firm the ground around the stem with your heel, water well, and tie to stake. Surprising materials make suitable tree ties. Old pairs of tights or stockings make great tree ties as they are flexible yet strong. Tie them in a figure of eight between the tree and stake to protect the stem from rubbing on the stake. You need to make sure the tree ties do not rub or harm the tree. Replace them as the tree grows so that they do not bind the tree too tightly.

Deciduous trees are best planted when they are resting between autumn and spring. Try to avoid planting in frosty or waterlogged soil. Evergreens are best planted in warm soil, in autumn or spring. Although container-grown trees can be planted at any time of year, it is still best to stick to the correct season if you can.

If your garden is generally dry, you could create a shallow depression around a new tree so that, when you water it, the water doesn't run away. In wet areas, it may be better to make a slight hump to improve drainage.

When planting soft fruit, take extra effort to ensure that the ground is completely free of perennial weeds. Leave two months between preparation of your soil and planting in the autumn. This way you will see if any weeds are still active.

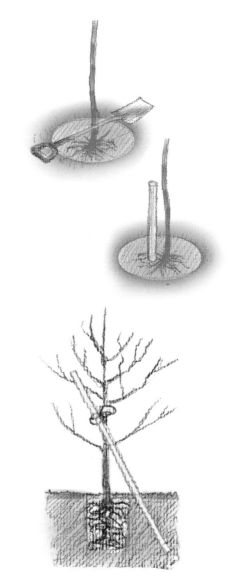

Planting a bare-rooted tree
Start by getting someone to hold the tree in position to be sure of the orientation and depth you want. Check the depth with your spade.

It is important that the hole is at least 4cm wider all round than the root spread.

To avoid damaging the roots, insert the stake off at an angle.

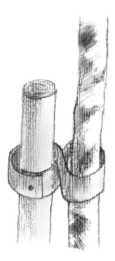

Attach the tree tie in a figure of eight to protect the trunk from rubbing on the stake.

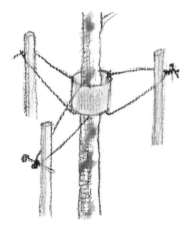

In areas of strong wind, secure the tree in three directions.

Permanent fruit and nut orchards can be underplanted with clumps of comfrey to cut and leave as nutritious mulch.

Tender loving care

Once your plants are growing in your wonderful soil, you need to keep a maternal eye on them. A regular stroll around the garden can make the difference between management as pleasure or chore. As you walk you might pick off a few pests, cut out or pull up one or two diseased plants, pull a few weeds, hitch up a trailing plant, collect some dried seed heads, pick some flowers, and harvest a few fresh fruits or vegetables for the table.

Keeping an eye on things is valuable, but every now and then you need to give your growing plants an extra boost to help them along. This is the time to use liquid fertilisers and foliar feeds.

Liquid fertiliser

Organic gardeners should always try and 'feed the soil, not the plants', but there is also a place for liquid fertilisers. They feed plants directly, providing them with readily accessible nutrients, and are most useful to boost plants while you are still building your soil's fertility. They also act as foliar feeds where roots are restricted, such as when plants are growing in containers.

COMFREY LIQUID

The most popular use of comfrey is in compost or as high potash liquid manure. If you have the space, place about 8 kilos of chopped comfrey in a 90-litre water butt, fill to the brim with water, and cover tightly. In about four weeks a liquid can be drawn off. Use this without diluting it as a general pick-me-up for potash-loving plants, or for anything that needs a tonic, even houseplants. Or you can make small batches of comfrey liquid in a plastic bucket. A few gardeners recommend using urine in place of some water for even higher nitrogen levels. Always cover a tub or bucket of comfrey liquid as the brew smells awful and also attracts flies and mosquitoes.

NETTLES AND HORSETAIL

Made in the same way as comfrey liquid, nettle leaf liquid makes a good general feed, high in major elements and magnesium, sulphur and iron. Horsetail is high in all soil nutrients, and rich in silica. Dilute these liquids about 10 to 1 and use them directly on plants.

Comfrey liquid made in drums. Draw it off into recycled plastic bottles for convenient use. The liquid has the rich colour of stout, but the fragrance of well-rotted pig manure.

Compost tea and liquids

Make this like liquid manure, or simply fill-half a bucket with compost and top up with water, cover it, and leave to steep for two weeks before diluting and using.

Compost tea makes an excellent pick-me-up for any tired plants, or as a boost to water seedlings or potted plants.

Comfrey liquid is excellent for tomatoes, peppers, aubergines, squashes and marrows, peas, beans, and soft fruit bushes.

Comfrey and nettle liquid are slightly alkaline and so are not recommended for acid-loving plants.

LIQUID MANURE

Fill a hessian sack with farmyard muck and suspend it in a barrel of water. After two weeks the liquid is ready to use. Liquid manure is a powerful plant food – never take it internally, use it sparingly on crops, and avoid spraying on the edible parts of plants.

LIQUID SEAWEED

Some commercial foliar feeds meet organic standards. Diluted and sprayed onto leaves, seaweed extract sustains chlorophyll levels, improves frost resistance, and stimulates a plant's immune response to pests and disease.

Watering

Water is essential for good plant growth and it is usually needed most during the season with least rainfall, so you will at some point need to supply your plants with water. It is important to water thoroughly rather than little and often. This good soaking encourages plants to put down deep roots to find the water they need.

Fresh rain water is better than tap water in that it doesn't contain the array of artificial chemicals our drinking water contains. To store rain water effectively, make sure the water is enclosed and not left to stagnate.

Closely planted wide beds are more water-efficient than spaced rows.

Do not water during the heat of the day, as most will evaporate off the surface. Water, if you can, early in the morning.

Always water newly transplanted plants.

Interplant crops and ornamentals with similar watering requirements.

Some crops, such as tomatoes, need a lot of water in the heat of summer. A good way to get water to their roots is to bury an inverted plastic bottle or tube near to their roots. Fill this with water and allow the water to permeate the roots with no surface evaporation.

You can make dramatic water savings by planting moisture-loving, shade-tolerant salad crops in troughs between deeper-rooted crops such as beans and sweetcorn.

Harvesting and storing

Unlike the modern farmer, who selects varieties to mature at the same time and harvests his crop all at once, organic gardeners can take advantage of variations between individual plants, positions, and sowing times to extend their harvesting period as long as possible.

Some crops, like runner beans, mangetout peas, and asparagus can be picked in small, meal-sized quantities every few days over a period of many weeks. Others can be cut back and left to regrow so that they can be repeatedly harvested. Crops suitable for this cut-and-come-again regime include: chicory, sugar loaf, corn salad, cress, garden endive, some lettuces, spinach, oriental greens, salad rocket, and turnip tops. Even some mature crops, such as spring cabbage and winter lettuce, can be cut about 2 centimetres above the stump, rather than uprooted, and in the right conditions further heads develop. But however well you plan your planting and harvesting schedule you will inevitably end up with periods of excess. You can find many organic ways of storing your food crops and ornamentals.

LIVE STORAGE

The best way to preserve those essential phytochemicals and vitamins is to store your crops where they stand. Leeks, beetroots, parsnips, kohlrabi, and swedes can wait in the ground until you are ready to eat them. Winter cabbages can wait in the ground until the spring. Build up some protective soil around them or cover them lightly with straw to protect against the worst of the winter weather.

DRYING

Fruits, herbs, beans, and certain flowers dry well. Getting air to circulate sufficiently and reach the moist parts of the plant are essential. Herbs and flowers can be hung in small bunches in the shade. Fruit which contains a lot of moisture is best cut into slices before drying. Apples, for example, can be sliced in rings, threaded onto strings and dried in warm shade indoors. Onions are best dried outside on wire racks before storing.

Frozen peas retain almost all their nutritive value.

You can preserve many fruits, herbs, and vegetables in sugar, oil, alcohol, or vinegar.

Shell nuts before storing them in airtight jars.

Bottling and freezing both use a lot of energy and reduce the nutritional content of food. However, for some crops, such as tomatoes, bottling is an efficient method of long-term storage.

Above, garlic and onions can be stored after drying by plaiting their soft, dry stems together.

Right, allow squashes to air for a few days in the sun before storing indoors in a well-ventilated space.

weeds

*plants in the wrong place
at the wrong time*

weeds

Why should I know my weeds?

Although weeds are rarely deliberately invited into our gardens, they are usually unwanted, but this doesn't mean they are all undesirable. Some are useful to garden and gardener. There are dozens of definitions of weeds, from 'plants growing in the wrong place' to 'plants whose virtues have not yet been discovered'.

Some weeds are troublesome: they may host pests and diseases; they can smother your chosen plants; they will certainly compete for food, moisture, and light, and crowd out plants that you do want. Get to know your weeds. Once you appreciate their better qualities you will be more tolerant of them, able to spend less time weeding and more time enjoying other aspects of gardening.

Weeds only flourish when we make a place for them. A thriving well-managed garden will have few places for weeds as their job is to colonise bare land and open soil, to bring stability to disturbed sites so that no earth is left uncovered. They are one of nature's strategies for protecting bare soil and preventing erosion. When we cultivate the soil in our gardens we create an ideal environment for most weeds to get stuck in.

Unfortunately, weeds often like similar conditions to crop plants, but weeds are usually stronger – after all, they have survived for generations with only incidental help. Horsetail apparently existed in Jurassic times. But, like cultivated plants, there are some conditions weeds don't enjoy, and once you realise how they operate you can get rid of them.

Although you are gardening with nature as much as possible, you still want control over what grows in your garden. You may appreciate a colony of coltsfoot or rosebay willowherb as a beautiful patch of wildflowers in an open field; the white trumpet flowers of bindweed look glorious clambering over hedges or up trees, but they can become rampant in your garden.

A few weeds are poisonous. Some are a nuisance and you will need to find ways to discourage or eradicate them. Fortunately, there are plenty of effective organic techniques for weed control. On the other hand, some weeds actually help to keep garden and gardener healthy. So before you rush to discover ways to uproot them all, always remember that some plants that are seen as weeds are actually useful additions to your garden.

Common garden weeds

ANNUALS
Black medick *(Medicago lupulina)*
Chickweed *(Stellaria media)*
Cleavers *(Galium aparine)*
Corn spurrey *(Spergula arvensis)*
Corncockle *(Agrostemma githago)*
Cranesbill *(Geranium spp.)*
Fat hen *(Chenopodium album)*
Field pansy *(Viola arvensis)*
Field poppy *(Papaver rhoeas)*
Fumitory *(Fumaria officinalis)*
Groundsel *(Senecio vulgaris)*
Hairy bittercress *(Cardamine hirsute)*
Hairy vetch *(Vicia hirsute)*
Hedge mustard *(Sisymbrium officinale)*
Henbit *(Lamium amplexicaule)*
Herb Robert *(Geranium robertianum)*
Himalayan balsam *(Impatiens grandiflora)*
Knotgrass *(Polygonum aviculare)*
Nipplewort *(Lapsana communis)*
Pineapple mayweed *(Matricaria perforate)*
Scarlet pimpernel *(Anagallis arvensis)*
Shepherd's purse *(Capsella bursapastoris)*
Sowthistle *(Sonchus oleraceus)*
Speedwell *(Veronica spp.)*
Sun spurge *(Euphorbia helioscopia)*
Yellow oxalis *(Oxalis corniculata)*

Cleavers

Groundsel

Himalayan balsam

Borage

Common ragwort

Chickweed seedlings, groundsel, lemon balm and tomato colonise an idle vegetable bed.

BIENNIALS
Burdock *(Arctium lappa)*
Garlic mustard *(Alliaria petiolata)*
Ragwort *(Senecio jacobaea)*
Teasel *(Dipsacus fullonum)*

PERENNIALS
Bindweed *(Convolvulus arvensis)*
Bracken *(Pteridium aquilinum)*
Coltsfoot *(Tussilago farfara)*
Comfrey *(Symphytum officinale)*
Couch grass *(Agropyron repens)*
Cow parsley *(Anthriscus sylvestris)*
Creeping buttercup *(Ranunculus repens)*
Creeping cinquefoil *(Potentilla repens)*
Creeping thistle *(Cirsium arvense)*
Dandelion *(Taraxacum officinale)*
Dock *(Rumex spp.)*
Field garlic *(Allium vineale)*
Greater celandine *(Chelidonium majus)*
Ground elder *(Aegopodium podagraria)*
Ground ivy *(Glechoma hederacea)*
Hedge bindweed *(Calystegia sepium)*
Horsetail *(Equisetum arvensis)*
Ivy *(Hedera helix)*
Lesser Celandine *(Ranunculus ficaria)*
Nettle *(Urtica dioica)*
Oxalis *(Oxalis articulate)*
Plantain *(Plantago major)*
Rosebay willowherb *(Epilobium angustifolium)*
Selfheal *(Prunella vulgaris)*
Silverweed *(Potentilla anserine)*
Toadfiax *(Linaria vulgaris)*
White deadnettle *(Lamium album)*
Yarrow *(Achillea millefolium)*

What use are weeds?

Weeds can tell you about your soil and may even help to improve or stabilise it. They make nutritious compost, they can attract helpful creatures, they may be edible, or they may benefit the health of garden or gardener.

1

Elements found in common weeds:

Yarrow
iron, calcium, potassium, copper, phosphorus, nitrogen, sulphur

Couch grass
potassium, silicon, chlorine, molybdenum

Mayweed
iron, calcium, phosphorus, sulphur

Stinging nettle
calcium, copper, iron, potassium, nitrogen

Dandelion
iron, sodium, potassium, phosphorus

Bracken
nitrogen, potassium, phosphorus

Horsetail (1)
potassium, phosphorus, cobalt, calcium, silicon, iron, magnesium

Silverweed (2)
iron, calcium, magnesium

2

3

Weeds as soil indicators:

Fertile soils
4

chickweed
nettle
cleavers
deadnettle
borage
speedwell
redshank
sun spurge (3)
creeping thistle
fumitory
sowthistle
stinging nettle
dandelion
groundsel

5

Acid soils
corn spurrey
sorrel
plantain
knotgrass

Alkaline soils
field pansy
field mouse ear
poppy (5)
charlock

6

Generally poor soils
poppies
dock

Compacted soils
grasses
greater plantain (4)
pineapple mayweed
silverweed

Too much nitrogen
cow parsley

Too little nitrogen
vetches
clovers
medick

Poorly drained soils
horsetail
creeping buttercup
silverweed
coltsfoot
dock
ragged robin
butterwort
bog pimpernel
sedges
mosses (6)

What do weeds do for my soil?

Many weeds have the advantages of being sturdier and more deep-rooted than their cultivated companions. While this can be irritating in borders and beds where they are competing for resources with cultivated plants, it is extremely useful in poor and bare soils.

PREVENTING SOIL EROSION

When you leave any patch of soil bare, the weather will work at it to destroy the structure, and wash or blow away the nutrients plants need. When rain falls onto bare clay soil it causes puddling – areas where water gathers without draining away. This compacts the soil so air can't get into it, and water can't drain through it and it becomes increasingly infertile – the more compacted the soil structure, the less nutrition can get in or out of the soil. When rain falls onto bare, sandy soil it washes the top layers away, sometimes exposing the subsoil where topsoil layers are thin. Even the best loam soils suffer from weathering if they are left bare.

Weeds naturally colonise bare soil. You know you have serious problems if weeds do not take over a patch of bare soil, as this suggests it is not in a condition where even the toughest plants are tempted to live.

As they cover the ground, their roots help to improve both the structure of the soil and the nutrition within it. Weeds are opportunists – they are used to digging around to find what they need, unlike most cultivated plants, which expect their needs to be catered for. If what they need isn't immediately available, they search for it. This is why some weeds have such well-developed branching roots, giving them the best chance of finding the food they need, whatever the condition of the soil.

The root systems of many grasses, including the detested couch grass, can travel many metres, with no respect for other plants that might get in their way: if you grow root vegetables in a plot infested with couch grass don't be surprised to dig up your crop to find couch grass roots growing right through them.

But this isn't all bad news. If you have to leave a patch of couch grass for a year or so before attending to it, it will have spread dramatically and take longer to remove, but as it spreads it leaves hundreds of fine channels in the soil, where its roots ran. So it leaves the soil better aerated and therefore, with improved drainage, particularly in a heavy soil.

Black medick is a legume, so it will increase available nitrogen in your soil.

It used to be traditional practice to store apples on slatted trays lined with nettle leaves. This is reputed to keep the fruit from rotting.

DON'T WEED — INCREASE FERTILITY

Organic gardeners often grow green manure. They are sown expressly to prevent leaving soil bare, and to increase fertility when they are incorporated into the soil. When the crop is mature, and before it flowers, dig it in to the ground or cut and leave it on top of the soil as a mulch.

Annual weeds can fulfil the same purpose if you don't have time to clear the ground and sow green manure. Treat them in the same way as any cover crop — never let them flower and set seed or you will increase your problems immeasurably. While growth is fairly lush, cut them down and fork them into the top few centimetres of soil. Then you are preventing erosion, adding nutrition to the soil through the nutrients the plants will have stored in their leaves and stems, and adding organic matter to the soil to increase the activity of soil life. Or you can cut and compost them.

If clovers, vetches, or black medick colonise areas of your garden, even in flower and vegetable beds, leave them in the ground for as long as you can, as they increase available nitrogen in your soil. When you weed them out, leave them on the surface for earthworms and other soil organisms to incorporate them into the soil.

The benefits of deep-feeders

Shallow-rooted cultivated plants feed predominantly in the top 20 centimetres of soil, so they will only be able to flourish when the soil is well tended, with plenty of organic matter incorporated where they need it. Deep-rooted plants raise plant foods from deep in the soil and make them available to shallow-feeders. At the same time as they mine deep into the subsoil, they are opening up the soil, creating channels for aeration and water.

Don't be too hard on docks. They are not hard to pull or dig out when soil is slightly moist, and they do an excellent job of stabilising eroded or otherwise damaged soil. Their deep roots mine the subsoil for nutrients, while the large fleshy leaves yield large amounts of organic matter when they decay onto the soil. The related fat hen also makes calcium and iron available to other plants.

A garden full of nettles looks initially daunting, but nettles are busy bringing up numerous minerals and trace elements from the soil. Some of the most fertile soil in your garden will be where you have removed an established patch of nettles. Dandelions can become a bit of a pest; easy to remove from beds, but troublesome in lawns and producing thousands of seeds. But they too are busy mining the soil for nutrients, bringing up significant quantities of iron, copper, and potassium.

Comfrey can be an invasive weed in damp gardens, but it is a wonderful source of nutrients. The main roots of a comfrey plant can be 7 centimetres in diameter at the base, and will happily push 2 metres down in the soil to bring up large quantities of plant foods and trace elements. Never eradicate comfrey, as it is one of the most useful plants in an organic garden, because of the number of nutrients it accumulates, and its speed of growth and decomposition. Horsetail is also found in damp places, throwing up fruiting spores in spring, followed by bristly upright stems. It is another greedy plant that brings to the surface whatever nutrients it can find.

Weeds in the compost

Don't throw weeds out, instead spread them to dry on the soil where you have hoed or pulled them out, or compost them. Everything they have taken out of the soil can be returned to it, with interest, via your compost heap.

Don't worry about incorporating some annual weed seeds. You can weed them out later. Even the most invasive perennial weed roots, such as ground elder, will compost if they are thoroughly dried for a week or two in the sun, or well-rotted in a sealed plastic sack. Test they are not still alive by scattering some moist soil over them.

Bracken is an invasive weed in some areas, but an excellent addition to the compost heap, providing plenty of swift-rotting bulk as well as plenty of plant foods. Chop it when it is green and still high in nutrients.

Horsetail is another weed that composters should seek out. As well as secreting high levels of potassium and phosphorus, this ancient plant accumulates high levels of cobalt, calcium, and silica which stimulate activity in a compost heap.

Several varieties of spurge are persistent annual weeds, irritating because some people are allergic to their milky sap. When they grow they rob the soil of boron, which is returned through composting. Sun spurge is most valuable as it steals most trace elements from the soil, but all spurges help to maintain the temperature of a compost heap. Yarrow is another greedy plant, accumulating copper and useful amounts of phosphorus, potassium, and calcium, which it gives up speedily into a compost heap.

Above, all weeds, even those with seriously aggressive root systems, can be composted. Dry invasive perennials first in the sun, or leave them to rot for several weeks in a black plastic sack before adding them to a heap.

As you cultivate your garden, horsetail will gradually disappear because it won't survive in very fertile soil. It is an interesting and ancient plant, so consider leaving a small patch to mine for nutrients in a damp area – harvest it twice a year for compost.

It takes persistence to get rid of couch grass, but when you dig it up, be sure it is destined for the compost heap. Its roots contain high levels of potassium, silica, chlorine, and various trace elements, which it steals from the ground as it grows. Dry roots for several weeks before chopping them up small and adding them to your compost heap. It is wise to replenish the ground where you have removed couch grass with compost containing the weed. This also seems to deter any couch rootlets that remain.

Deep-feeding weeds store considerable reserves of food in their roots so they are always valuable additions to compost. Spread dandelion, teasel, and dock roots to dry before adding them. They are all more nutritious when they are young and must be cut for compost before they set seed.

Weeds as companions

Stinging nettles aren't popular additions to a garden border or vegetable bed, but leave a few round the edge of your vegetable beds. They host nettle aphids to feed early-waking ladybirds in spring. When they grow near tomatoes, the fruits will ripen more quickly and be less likely to rot; black, red, and white currants will crop more heavily, herbs will produce more oils. Yarrow is another stimulant that helps neighbouring plants to grow more strongly.

Some weeds like to grow hand-in-hand with cultivated plants – yields of wheat are actually improved by small numbers of corncockles, mayweed, or white mustard. But crops are choked if weeds get out of hand, so they should be weeded out at crucial early stages of crop growth.

Plants with a wide leaf spread, such as fat hen, are useful in your vegetable bed, if kept under control. Their deep roots bring minerals to the soil surface, and their wide leaf spread keeps the ground moist and shaded for seedlings.

Weeds and wildlife

A weed-free garden would be rather an unfriendly place for wildlife. Because weeds are such adaptable survivors, one or other is likely to be flowering at almost any time of year, providing food or nectar for animals and insects when there may be little choice. They may also help to keep wild creatures from eating your cultivated plants.

Bad companions:

Creeping buttercups and other members of the Ranunculaceae family make poor neighbours, as the secretions from their roots poison nitrogen-fixing bacteria in the soil so that other plants suffer.

Fat hen and docks attract aphids. Chickweed attracts whitefly and red spider mite, so should be cleared from glasshouses and tunnels in particular.

One of a weed's most important roles is to attract pest predators into your garden. Once you realise that nettles, nipplewort, and even bindweed attract ladybirds and hoverflies, and therefore help keep aphids under control, you'll probably be happy to host a few. Similarly, ground beetles gravitate towards creeping thistle, ground elder, and chickweed, from where they venture out to eat pest insects and even slugs and snails. Hoverflies are attracted to cow parsley. A very tidy garden doesn't provide the support and hiding places that these important predators need.

Sowthistle attracts birds and insects, and this mineral-rich plant is an excellent addition to any animal's diet – vets use it to help problems with high blood pressure and heart disorders. It is also a useful trap plant. It is host to leafminers and aphids, and should be left in the ground until early summer, then pulled up and composted. Clovers host beneficial insects, particularly predators of woolly aphis, so they are particularly useful left growing among apple trees. Clovers also provide good cover for the ground beetles, which prey on slugs and snails.

Ivy can be a nuisance, but leave some on walls or trees to provide shelter for birds, and butterflies will hibernate in its green depths. It also provides late autumn flowers for bees to build up stores of pollen for the winter. Ivy on the ground hosts many helpful beetles, and its deep cover makes a good hiding place for frogs and some useful small mammals.

Groundsel is another valuable animal food – it was once grown as a crop to feed pigs, goats, rabbits, and poultry, to add iron to their diet. In some European countries couch grass is still harvested specially for horse and cattle food, because it is so rich in minerals.

If you can keep them under control, blackberries are a favourite nectar plant for butterflies and make good cover for birds, as well as providing useful food.

Eat your weeds

Weeds spread hand-in-hand with human activity, and humans have always found uses for the commonest ones. Medicines were originally made from wild plants, and weeds were often valued as food. When you are weeding your garden, save some for the pot – vegetables all developed from once-wild plants, and many weeds are very nutritious. Nettles are rich in vitamins A and C as well as minerals, and young leaves make a tasty as well as healthy soup.

Free food: sorrel (top) and blackberry.

Good food

Dandelions, poppies, bindweed, teasel, thistle, groundsel, chickweed, plantain, knotgrass, and sowthistle provide food for a range of wildlife.

Bindweed, brambles, fat hen, thistle, ivy, clover, deadnettles, campion, medick, and goldenrod are useful nectar plants for butterflies.

Bees love the flowers of corncockle, clovers, cranesbill, forget-me-not, groundsel, ivy, meadowsweet, ox-eye daisies, poppies, bird's-foot trefoil, valerian, and yarrow.

Dandelion leaves contain significant levels of vitamin A, vitamin C, several B vitamins, and many minerals including calcium, chlorine, copper, iron, phosphorus, potassium, magnesium, silicon, and sulphur. Not bad for a weed! Eat young dandelion leaves in salads or pick the whole crown and blanch it for a minute in boiling water to take away any bitterness, then change the water and cook as spinach.

Fat hen is often cooked as a spinach-type vegetable; it contains more B vitamins and iron and protein than raw cabbage or spinach, and plenty of calcium. But always pick young plants, as older ones store high levels of oxalic acid. If you don't manage to get rid of all your ground elder, brought to England by the Romans as a pot herb, weaken what remains by regularly picking leaves for the pot – they taste quite pleasant with butter.

SALADS

Wild sorrel is the same as cultivated, but it will be very acid if growing in acid soils, in which case, use it as a cooked vegetable rather than as salad greens. Like fat hen, use only young leaves because it also contains oxalic acid. Chickweed was once sold on city streets as cress. It is a useful salad plant because it is one of the few herbs that contains significant amounts of copper, often lacking in our diet. Hairy bittercress is another useful addition to the salad bowl and the leaves of garlic mustard add a pleasant hot garlic flavour.

Stinging nettles act as an anti-histamine and are used by medical herbalists to treat rheumatoid arthritis, hay fever, and asthma.

Left, dandelion is used by medical herbalists as a powerful diuretic and contains many beneficial phytochemicals. One of these, inulin, feeds beneficial bacteria in the gut and is proven to protect against certain cancers.

How do I control the weeds that I don't want?

First, understand how weeds spread.

Seeds

All garden soil is a huge bank of weed seeds, some dormant, some ready to germinate. Weeds are survivors, and plants often produce vast quantities of seeds – one fat hen plant can drop around half a million seeds in a good year. All annual and some perennial weeds spread by seed, so you should always try and remove the flower heads before they set seed. But hundreds of thousands more will blow in, or arrive on passing animals, carried by birds, on the soles of your shoes, or brought by visitors.

Some seeds are designed to travel, others to stay put. Coltsfoot, nipplewort and many others have tiny seeds that blow about easily. Dandelion, groundsel, and thistle seeds blow about with the help of tiny parachutes. Willowherbs have hairs to catch the wind, sycamore trees have winged seeds like helicopters. Blackberry seeds need to travel so plants can colonise new areas, and they germinate most easily after passing through a bird's gut. Cleavers and burdock seeds have velcro-like hooks to grab on to passing animals' coats. Shepherd's purse seeds, oxalis, and Himalayan balsam explode out of their seed pods at the slightest touch, and are often inadvertently spread through weeding.

Roots, runners, and rhizomes

Hardy perennial weeds do produce seeds, but these are often just for back-up as they also spread vegetatively. Weeds with tap roots have a large, simple or branched storage root. A new plant will grow from even the tiniest piece of root left in the ground or cut up when you are digging or cultivating the ground. Some of the most invasive weeds, including couch grass and ground elder also spread from segments of root. Additionally, they have long, branching rhizomes or roots under the ground so they can spread over 8–10 sqare metres in one season.

Bindweed spreads rampantly above ground, strangling other plants that it uses as support. With other aggressive weeds, including coltsfoot, it grows equally rampantly beneath the surface, sending down deep-spreading roots that regrow whenever top sections are removed. One root of bindweed can develop over one season into a network reaching a terrifying 25 sqare metres. Horsetail is almost as

Night time cultivation
As seeds need light to germinate, research suggests that cultivating and weeding at night may reduce weed problems. This may reduce germination of a few varieties, but most weed seeds in the top centimetre of soil still receive enough light to germinate.

Chickweed, fat hen, dock, and sowthistle host pest insects.

Groundsel, shepherd's purse, and chickweed spread viral diseases. Charlock and shepherd's purse transmit club root.

The flowers and seeds of ragwort and corncockle are poisonous.

Groundsel and foxglove seedlings are poisonous – so be careful to remove them from salad beds, where they could be mistakenly picked with a crop.

Always be careful with gifts of plants from friends' and neighbours' gardens. Check the roots of the plants very carefully and remove any hints of runners or rhizomes before planting.

Weeds are designed to survive. It is estimated that 25 per cent of all weed seeds will germinate 10 years after being buried in the soil at depths below 2m. Some remain viable for centuries.

Regular weeding is the way to success, but it is better to hand-weed as often as you can rather than hoe excessively as this can damage the soil's structure. Light hoeing once every two or three weeks is plenty, but you can hand-weed whenever you like.

Hoes are most useful where you can weed between lines of vegetables, so mark your rows with string before you sow. If young seedlings are out of line they risk being beheaded with the weeds when you hoe.

active. Creeping buttercup and wild strawberry run along the ground, producing plantlets at regular intervals which put down roots and send out more runners. Blackberries can shoot 1 metre a week in summer, sending stem roots to develop into more plants.

The best line of attack is always prevention, and good soil management will control weeds in time. Even persistent problems, such as horsetail, will disappear as soil becomes more fertile. Cultivate carefully; time spent in eradicating weeds when they first appear is time well spent.

Hoeing and hand-weeding

TIMING

The most critical period of weed control is the four weeks following germination of your planted seeds. After that, weeds can still interfere with your plants. They may look unsightly and can harbour unwanted pests and diseases, but your plants will have a good chance of surviving any competition. So if you only manage to keep weeds under control for that critical time, from late spring to early summer, you'll have gone a long way to help the productivity in your garden.

You need to get your timing right to be successful in the war against perennials. They depend on stores of food in their large roots or tubers, and if you hoe them off in spring the roots will simply regenerate. It is best to smother them or dig them out, or hit strong weeds with the hoe when they are weakest – when they're just about to flower. Then their food reserves are at their lowest.

TOOLS

The most useful tools for weed control are a handfork and a hoe. A hoe cuts weeds off from their roots just below the soil surface, and is most useful for keeping the ground clear between rows of plants.

Small weeds and larger annuals can be pulled out by hand, using a handfork to help you ease the plant out where necessary. Follow an old adage and 'pull when wet, hoe when dry'. If you try and pull weeds out by hand when the soil is very dry, the roots will simply break off and remain in the ground. In wet soil you can pull up even long taproots without difficulty, and without major disturbance to the surrounding ground.

Perennial spreaders

Tap roots and seed
Comfrey *(Symphytum officinale)*
Cow parsley *(Anthriscus Sylvestris)*
Dandelion *(Taraxacum officinale)*
Dock *(Rumex spp)*.
Teasel *(Dipsacusfullonum)*

Runners above ground
Blackberry *(Rubusfruticosa)*
Creeping buttercup *(Ranunculus repens)*
Creeping cinquefoil *(Potentilla reptans)*
Ground ivy *(Glechoma hederacea)*
Selfheal *(Prunella vulgaris)*
Silverweed *(Potentilla anserine)*
Wild strawberry *(Fragaria vesca)*

Shallow-running roots
Couch grass *(Agropyron repens)*
Ground elder *(Aegopodium podagraria)*
Nettle *(Urtica dioica)*
Rosebay willowherb *(Epilobiurn angustifolium)*

Deep-spreading roots
Bindweed *(Convolvulus arvensis)*
Coltsfoot *(Tussilagofarfara)*
Creeping thistle *(Cirsium arvense)*
Hedge bindweed *(Calystegia sepium)*
Horsetail *(Equisetum arvensis)*
Ivy *(Hedera helix)*

Corms or bulbils
Lesser Celandine *(Ranunculusficaria)*
Oxalis *(Oxalis articulate)*

Stinging nettle

Ground elder

Dandelion

Creeping buttercup

Try to stagger your planting through the seasons so you can keep up with any weeding that does need attending to. Even if you're not growing winter vegetables, crops such as garlic can be planted in autumn to get established over winter and early spring before weeds take hold.

You can plant ground-cover plants to prevent weeds emerging, but be careful what you choose. Many ground-cover plants such as periwinkles (Vinca spp.) or St John's Wort (Hypericum perforatum) can themselves become invasive weeds.

Vinca minor

Regular hoeing is a good way of keeping beds clear of all but heavy weed growth. But you need dry weather for hoeing so that every weed you dislodge will die straight away and so that the weeds you leave on the surface will shrivel and die fast.

Several types of hoe exist and gardeners usually develop personal preferences. A Dutch hoe, sometimes called a 'push' hoe, has a blade which is sharp on the lower edge, and a two-edged hoe is sharpened on both edges. These have a gap between the blade and the handle so that weeds and soil pass over the hoe's blade as you move it backwards and forwards just beneath the surface of the soil, chopping off any plants it meets. The blade of a draw hoe is attached directly to the handle, and this is used on the soil's surface to chop off larger weeds. You can also purchase short-handled draw hoes, sometimes called onion hoes, for weeding in small areas.

SPADE OR FORK?

Only use a spade for initial ground clearance. It is counterproductive to try and dig out weeds with long runners and rhizomes that appear in the middle of cultivated plants. Every tiny bit of root that remains in the ground will grow into another plant. You must pull them out carefully, using hands and a hand fork, or a fork if the problem is sizeable. If weed roots are tangled around established plants, you will need to remove those plants and disentangle any runners from their roots before replanting.

FLAME WEEDING

Flame weeding can be useful for removing weeds in some places, such as on stony paths and walls where you can't hoe and weeds won't budge with hand-weeding. You don't burn the weeds to a crisp – just pass a flame over them until they change to a darker green, which shows that their cells walls have burst. But flame weeding is slow. You may need to keep attacking the weeds every few days for a week or two. And it is costly – you must buy a proprietary flame weeder, never make your own.

Planting to outwit weeds

Don't be put off gardening because you haven't the time or energy to clear all your weeds before you plant; sometimes you may have to find other ways to manage a weedy plot. While some plants are very susceptible to competition, others will survive and even flourish.

GREEN MANURES FOR WEED SUPPRESSION

All cover crops suppress weed growth, and grazing rye also acts as a natural herbicide, producing toxins from its roots that kill many weed seeds and seedlings, even couch grass. However, when the foliage is turned into the soil this can prevent small seeds germinating, so follow rye with large, seeded vegetables such as beans, and wait to sow until three to four weeks after digging in the plants.

Smothering weeds

You can use any organic matter for a sheet mulch to keep weeds at bay, or combine it with sheets of newsprint or cardboard. Whatever sheet method you choose, always improve your soil properly before laying the sheet mulch; once a mulch is in place it's hard to get at the soil to replenish soil life. You can plant shrubs, trees, perennials, and most vegetable seedlings through carpet, cardboard, newspaper, and porous plastic.

BARRIERS

If your garden has a perennial weed problem, chances are your neighbours will have one as well. To avoid weeds spreading, clear them from the edges of your property and dig a trench about 45 centimetres deep and 15 wide at any boundary, or beneath a dividing fence. Line it with heavy-duty polythene, or bricks, slates, or tiles. If you're faced with a very weedy garden, and you want to get growing quickly, build raised beds (see page 95). Even raising a bed 15 centimetres above ground level can help control weeds.

SOIL STRATEGIES

If you manage your soil well you should have few weed problems. Maintain high levels of organic matter in your soil, keep an eye on drainage, and test the pH regularly to ensure you give your plants the best chances by growing them in the conditions they prefer. Practising rotation (see page 89) in a vegetable bed helps keep your soil healthy, and therefore prevents weeds from getting established as well as deterring pests and diseases.

Potatoes have traditionally been used as ground-clearers, and other greedy feeders, such as squash, also leave the ground fairly weed-free for other crops to follow. They also suppress weeds because of their generous leaf spread, so you can follow them with crops that are more vulnerable to weed competition, such as peas and beans.

Always mulch soil when it is warm and moist, but not wet. Too wet and the mulch prevents it drying out, so the ground gets waterlogged; too dry and the mulch may prevent it ever getting wet enough, as moisture filters slowly through a mulch.

Use beech or oak leaves, or even pine needles, to suppress weeds on strawberry beds, as strawberries like the acid conditions this creates. If organic mulch is not well-rotted, you must rake it off before cultivation as it will take a population explosion of bacteria in the soil to decompose and incorporate it, and they will use up available nitrogen for their own development, causing a shortage in the soil. Well-rotted matter is easily assimilated.

Use black plastic mulches to clear land and eradicate stubborn perennial weeds. Once you have cleared the plot, you can re-lay porous mulches and plant through them, or use them as mats around fruit trees and shrubs.

Never use hay as a weed-suppressing mulch as it often brings thousands of weed seeds with it.

If you use tomatoes to clear an infestation of couch grass, don't cultivate potatoes or tomatoes the following year otherwise you risk the build-up of pests or diseases in the soil.

Fat hen

Mulches

All sheet mulches must be firmly pegged with stakes or weighted down with stones.

Weed suppressing mulches:
Annual weed problems
compost
muck
straw
autumn leaves
grass mowings
mushroom compost
newspaper with any of the above

Perennial problems
thick carpet
black plastic
cardboard with organic matter

Maintenance
Top up levels of organic mulch regularly, pulling out any weeds that appear.

Place porous plastic mats around trees and shrubs in grassland and orchards.

PLANT WARS

Some weeds inhibit the growth of cultivated plants by excreting substances in their roots or flowers. Fat hen, for example, releases toxic levels of oxalic acid into the soil when it starts flowering, to inhibit the growth of any neighbouring plants. Creeping buttercups and others release substances that poison nitrogen-fixing bacteria in the soil so other plants become deficient.

Fortunately, some cultivated plants have similar effects on weeds. Plant tomatoes in areas of your garden troubled by couch grass. Use them as sacrificial plants even where you can't expect to harvest the fruits, as their root excretions can deter vigorous infestations of the weed. Simply turn the couch-ridden area over to one spade's depth in early summer, throw some good topsoil or planting compost between the upturned clods and heel in young tomato plants – use a vigorous variety such as Broad Yellow ripple currant, which itself grows wild as a weed in some areas of the southern United States. Compost the tomato plants in autumn and mulch the ground over winter. The following season your ground should be couch-free.

The African marigold (*Tagetes minuta*) seems also to excrete powerful herbicides from its roots. Start seeds indoors to be sure of successful germination, and plant strong seedlings into ground infested with persistent perennial weeds such as bindweed, ground elder, and horsetail. Provided the young plants get established, they should suppress all but the most serious infestation. Marigolds only seem to have an effect on plants with starchy roots, so they can be safely planted near woody-rooted plants such as shrubs, roses, and soft fruit. Keep them out of herbaceous borders and only plant them round the edge of vegetable beds or they may inhibit, or even destroy, some plants you want, along with weeds.

Weeds in paths and walls

You should never need to waste time weeding where you walk – a path that takes a lot of foot traffic rarely has a chance to get weedy, so a weedy path may mean you don't really need a path at all. Stepping stones through a border may serve as well, or turn a weedy path through lawn back into grass, insetting some slabs if you wish. Slabs in grass must be at ground level for easy mowing.

Whatever path you choose, make sure it is laid well – concrete, slabs and pavers are then very resistant to weeds. Paths made of old bricks or slabs are attractive, but it can be hard to uproot weeds by hand, so if they get very weedy you should either repeatedly flame weed, or preferably lift and relay them. Dig the path out to at least 20 centimetres below ground level, fill the bottom 8 centimetres with gravel and cover this with a thick layer of sand under the bricks or slabs. This prevents weeds from seeding and rooting and provides drainage. Then brush a dry mix of sand and cement into cracks between paving slabs so weeds can't develop.

Gravel paths are easier to weed – you can use a hoe in severe cases, or hand-weed. You can scatter seeds of attractive ornamentals on gravel, or plant some herbs. If you want a plant-free path, spread a layer of porous plastic at the bottom of the 20-centimetre trench, then fill with gravel. Edge paths with wood or vertical stones to avoid grass and weeds spreading from lawns or borders.

Weedy walls

If dry stone walls get really covered in ivy or full of creeping perennial weeds you ought to take them apart and rebuild them, if at all possible. But weeds such as creeping Jenny and herb Robert look attractive clambering out of walls, and most annuals can be easily pulled out without harming the wall. Ivy is fine climbing strong walls, but it delights in pushing into weak and crumbling mortar, and can damage or destroy weak walls, so pull it out carefully.

Weedy lawns

A weedy lawn probably means a problem with your soil. If you inherit a thoroughly weedy lawn it is best to remove the turf, stack it to rot into loam, and improve the soil before resowing. Remove weeds, check the pH of the soil and add lime if it is at all acid. Then dig in plenty of compost or organic matter to improve structure and fertility, with extra topsoil if necessary to build up the soil level. Prepare a seed bed and resow, choosing a suitable grass seed mixture – meadow grasses grow in the shade; rye grass is hard wearing.

If resowing is not an option, hand-weed plantains, dandelions, and any other weeds with large flat leaves that smother the grass. Remove creeping buttercups as they suppress grass and clover growth. Ease lawn weeds out carefully with an old kitchen knife or fine trowel. Sprinkle finely ground lime or powdered seaweed if pH is acid. Encourage healthy growth with regular mowing, leaving clippings on the grass to feed the lawn and encourage earthworms.

Weeds will do better than grass in very wet or very dry areas, so keep your lawn well-drained and moss-free by raking out patches of

Paths in vegetable beds

Pathways covered in an organic material such as bark chippings are ideal for a vegetable garden, and are easy to maintain. If they get weedy hoe them or dig them in and start again. But don't use old hay as it contains weed seeds and can aggravate problems.

Use an old kitchen knife to weed between bricks and slabs, slipping the blade down to chop weeds as near the roots as possible. Or take hold of the top of the weed firmly and pull very gently to ease it out; never let weeds in paths flower and set seed.

If an old brick or paved path is very hard to keep weed-free, sow annual flower seeds in any gaps to compete with the weeds.

Except in a very large garden, never plant **mints** (*Mentha spp.*) or **horseradish** (*Armoracia rusticana*) in an open bed. Instead, grow them in buried containers.

Be careful when choosing ornamental plants for **ground cover**. Their nature is to cover ground quickly and effectively and virtually any ground-cover plant can become an invasive nuisance.

Soil pH is crucial to a healthy lawn, which depends on earthworm activity to drag down any rotting matter and prevent build-up of thatch. Earthworms will not survive if the pH is below 5.5.

Topdressing keeps a lawn in good condition and therefore discourages weeds. In early autumn scatter onto the lawn a mixture of compost and topsoil – finely worked molehill soil is perfect. This improves the surface structure and encourages earthworms.

Keep your lawn well-drained and moss-free by raking out patches of thatch.

Clover – a legume – nourishes the soil, improving your lawn.

thatch, and aerate compacted areas regularly by spiking them with your garden fork.

Helpful weeds

Some weeds can be encouraged to keep your lawn healthy – and attractive. Clovers maintain nitrogen levels, helping grass to stay lush and green; yarrow stays dark green in the driest weather; and creeping wild thyme (*Thymus serpyllum*) also withstands drought and has a beautiful scent. Daisies, bird's-foot trefoil and other wild flowers add interesting leaf shapes as well as flowers if you let them. The

Common lawn weeds

Dandelion (*Taraxacum officinale*)
Plantain (*Plantago major*)
Daisy (*Bellis perennis*)
Hawkweed (*Hieracium spp.*)
Yarrow (*Achillea millefolium*)
Cat's ear (*Hypochaeris radicata*)

This patch of lawn is almost smothered by creeping buttercup and daisies.

more you mow, the better the texture of your lawn becomes as weeds produce smaller and smaller leaves to become increasingly dense.

Invaders

Think hard before you invite some plants into your garden, as they can become invasive weeds in the garden and beyond. Japanese knotweed (*Polygonum cuspidatum*) was once a valued garden plant; it escaped and became so invasive that it is now illegal to plant it deliberately.

Borage has become a weed in many British gardens, but fortunately it is easy to control by removing flower heads before they seed; its perennial relative green alkanet (*Pentaglottis sempervirens*) spreads fast via seed and roots and has a deep tap root which regenerates itself if it is broken, so every shred needs to be removed. Fortunately alkanet is fast-decomposing and full of minerals, so it is a useful compost weed. Goldenrod (*Solidago officinalis*) can easily become another perennial pest with its aggressive root system and invasive habit – and it produces thousands of seeds. Keep its growth under check by dividing it each year and removing unwanted seedlings.

Tansy (*Tanacetum vulgaris*) is useful for attracting beneficial insects, and it may repel harmful ones, but its strong growth and huge seed production means it will speedily crowd out other plants very quickly. It is a helpful plant, but ideally you should grow it in containers so you can move it round the garden so other plants can enjoy its companion qualities without being devoured by it.

Jerusalem artichokes (*Helianthus tuberosus*) are vigorous perennial sunflowers with sprouting edible roots. They are valuable food plants, and their height (to 3m) means they can also be planted as useful weather shields, but keep their growing area contained by digging out all roots outside a chosen patch in late autumn. Never dig over a dormant patch of roots or you'll spread them everywhere.

If you buy wild strawberry plants (*Fragaria vesca*), be sure to get a named variety, otherwise your beds and lawn can quickly be taken over by this little creeping plant, which produces thousands of offsets and no fruits.

Japanese knotweed

Bird droppings can spread seeds and enable plants to flourish in tiny crevices, in this case a wild strawberry.

Don't worry about weeds

Every garden will have weeds, but they don't have to be a problem. Of course, it's ideal to spend time maintaining and enjoying your garden as often as you can throughout the year, but you may not always have the right amount of time at the right season. Even when you can't do as much as you might like, you can make sure your garden doesn't get overwhelmed by weeds, and you don't get overwhelmed by your garden.

YOUR GARDEN IS NOT A BATTLEGROUND

Make your garden the right size for you – the more space you cultivate, the more space for weeds, and the more difficult it is to keep on top of everything. And don't be impatient – never sow seeds or plant seedlings too early in spring or they will be subdued by competition from weeds that can happily cope with the conditions better than your chosen plants.

A good gardener must learn to relax – if you only have limited time to garden, and this coincides with wet or foul weather, do something else instead. Learn to love your weeds. Eat them, compost them or just appreciate them – once you think of hedge bindweed as white morning glory it can even seem beautiful!

Bindweed takes captive an idle fork.

pests

discriminate friend from foe

pests

Organic gardeners have enemies: pests that eat, damage, or disfigure food crops and beautiful ornamentals. Luckily, we also have allies working on side. The game plan is to encourage our allies and outwit our enemies.

As a garden is not a natural environment, pests can cause problems, but there are safe and effective ways to keep them from damaging your garden. It is always best to strike before any problem appears, and many natural ways of pest control are common sense practices, such as giving your plants the conditions they prefer. Some helpful planting schemes rely on centuries of gardeners' observations. Biological methods of control mimic processes at work in nature, and botanical pesticides break down without harming the environment. Or you can get physical and use traps and barriers.

Some insects breed incredibly fast – the common housefly can lay 600 eggs at a time, which hatch out in 6 days. So over the course of one summer one pair of flies could produce enough offspring to cover the whole surface of the Earth several layers thick. But this doesn't happen. Biological controls exist. You can take advantage of the natural cycles of pests and predators for pest control in your garden.

All insect pests have natural enemies. The use of these organisms to manage pests is known as biological control. The importance of pest predators should never be over-emphasised, and their conservation is a vitally important pest-control strategy in any garden.

Left, mini-wasps hatching out of a host cabbage caterpillar.

Cultivating a pest-free garden

Organic gardening means creating a garden that can help support itself, so the most important way of controlling pests is by good gardening practice.

Get the soil right

Choose plants that fit your site

Choose resistant varieties

Plant a mixture of species

Start plants in modules to give them a head start

Intercrop

Practise rotation

Clear the ground in autumn rather than leaving pests to overwinter on stumps of brassicas or in overwintering roots.

Always remove pest-affected leaves and vegetables and compost them in a hot heap rather than leaving them on the ground or on the plant.

Encouraging predators

Some predatory insects eat other insects; some use other insects as hosts, laying eggs in their bodies which hatch out, killing the host. Other creatures eat slugs and snails, or help keep soil healthy so that pests are less likely to get established. If you take a wide view, even so-called pests are beneficial in some way, as all creatures are part of complex food webs that support life on earth. So when we talk about beneficial garden insects, we mean 'beneficial to the gardener'. They won't completely rid your garden of pests, but they should stop any pest from getting out of control – and many predatory insects are also useful pollinators.

THE IMPORTANCE OF PREDATORS

Predatory insects are the lions and tigers of the insect world. They are voracious feeders, catching their prey and either crunching and chewing up their victims, or sucking out all their juices. The biological cycles of pests and predators will fit, given the right conditions in your garden. As a result, predators should appear at the time when your garden needs them most.

HABITATS

Most beneficial insects will appear naturally in your garden if you provide a diversity of plants and habitats. Keep your beds clear of decay that can host pests and diseases, but a very neat and tidy garden is an unwelcoming place for friends, so leave places for them to hibernate and hide. Get to know which creatures are most helpful; provide them with food, water, and a comfortable home.

Ladybirds, beetles, and centipedes

Most people know that ladybirds are good to have in your garden, because they eat greenfly and other aphids. Everybody recognises the adult black-spotted, red variety, but there are dozens of others including orange and yellow varieties with black spots and black ones with red spots. The larvae are less well known, but these small greyish-black grubs, with indistinct orange blotches, are the most voracious aphid eaters.

Ladybird feasts on aphid.

Varied planting encourages pollinators and predators. Plant annual flowers, such as marigolds, among vegetables, and edge beds with herbs.

Encourage birds by planting dense, native shrubs, and feed birds through the winter. They will eat hundreds of pests and their eggs.

A pond will bring in a range of aquatic life, including predatory dragonflies, frogs and toads.

A pile of logs offers protection or a place to hibernate for many garden helpers, including beetles, toads, frogs, slow worms, and hedgehogs.

Ground beetle

If pests such as aphids are abundant, ladybirds will tend to graze on them, skimming the top off the population, but not adequately suppressing them. So a diversity of predators is important, each with different feeding habits.

Centipedes eat small slugs as well as numerous insects. They are easy to tell apart from unhelpful millipedes as they scuttle very quickly and only have one pair of legs per body segment, while millipedes have two. Orange-brown, and usually around 2.5cm long, centipedes hide in dark, damp places and hunt at night.

Adult ladybirds hibernate in houses and hedgerows throughout the winter and then emerge to lay eggs in spring. One ladybird larva feeds for several weeks, eating up to 500 aphids before pupating and becoming an adult ladybird. As well as aphids, adult ladybirds eat mealybugs, scale insects, whiteflies, mites, and other insects.

OTHER BEETLES

Ground, or carabid, beetles are shiny purple-black beetles up to 2.5 centimetres long. You can find them among ground-cover plants, or hiding under rotting vegetation, or in mulches. They are mostly nocturnal, preying on slugs and caterpillars as well as smaller insects.

Hoverflies and lacewings

Ephemeral looking lacewings are among the most important insect predators in any garden. The adults are beautiful green or yellowish-green insects about 1.5 centimetres long, with gauze-like wings and golden eyes. An adult lives for 20 to 40 days, feeding on pollen and honeydew secreted by aphids. Every day each female lacewing lays 10 to 30 eggs on small stalks so that the later developers aren't eaten by the larvae that mature earlier. These pale brown larvae are incredibly active predators. They look like miniature flattened alligators and are known as 'aphid lions' because they eat so many aphids, along with spider mites, thrips, mealybugs, small caterpillars, and insect eggs.

HOVERFLIES

Hoverflies are also attractive insect predators, resembling small, slim wasps. They mimic the markings of bees and wasps to protect themselves from attack by birds, spiders, and other predators. But they are easy to tell apart as hoverflies are much smaller, hover steadily rather than darting up and down, and only have one pair of wings.

Like lacewings, adult hoverflies are nectar- and pollen-feeders and it is their larvae that gobble up aphids. These are brown or green, without jointed legs, and can often be found among aphid colonies, puncturing aphids' skin and sucking out the liquid contents.

A colony of aphids usually contains some aphid shells with holes pierced in one end. This is a sign that predatory larvae, such as those of the hoverfly (left), have been at work.

Lacewings and hoverflies are busy feeders and pollinators and particularly at risk from pesticides used on flowering plants. You can buy lacewing hotels to attract them into your garden, but they will only stay and breed if you include a good variety of attractant plants.

Birds and mammals, toads and frogs

Birds are both friends and pests, but they do more good than harm, so you should try to welcome them. Their habit of stealing your fruit, seeds, and young seedlings can drive you to distraction, but there are ways to foil them (see page 156), and they are also very helpful. Birds feed on hundreds of different pests at different stages of development – including troublesome pests such as slugs and snails, codling moth, cutworms, and wireworms, and they aerate the soil, where they pierce it with their beaks to seek insects.

BATS

If you have bats in your garden, don't scare them away. They will eat thousands of insects in one night, and their droppings make very rich fertiliser. They are also the most effective controllers of summer-biting insects such as mosquitoes and midges, as they come out to feed at about the time the biters get most active.

HEDGEHOGS

Hedgehogs are very greedy feeders – they eat slugs, millipedes, and many pest grubs, but they are not particularly choosy, and will also eat beneficial insects and even small mammals and birds' eggs. Encourage them into your garden with suitable hibernation sites such as log piles, but don't treat them as pets and feed them or they won't do their job as pest controllers. Hedgehogs love beer, so don't use beer traps (see page 151) when they're about.

TOADS AND FROGS

Try to provide frogs and toads with a pond, and some dark, damp places where they can hide and hibernate. Frogs feed predominantly off slugs, and toads also include numerous insects, woodlice, and ants in their diet. Toads and frogs burrow under plant material in the winter, or under upturned flower pots.

Don't destroy ants' nests as they are a favourite late-summer food of green woodpeckers.

People used to think that toads could give you warts, probably because of the bumps on toad skin that look like warts. These bumps contain poison that irritates the mouth of any predators who try to eat toads. Be careful in handling toads and always wash your hands afterwards.

Glow worms

Although increasingly rare, you sometimes see glow worms at the edge of fields or woodland, or at garden margins. These are beautiful little creatures, and also helpful, as their larvae live on slugs and snails.

Even ordinary garden wasps are excellent predators. To feed their young they can each catch over two hundred flies per hour.

Plant rows of beans between brassicas, and cabbage root fly and mealy aphids won't destroy a cabbage crop. This also seems to discourage blackflies from the beans. Plant sage or thyme near brassicas to put flea beetles off the scent.

Powdered wormwood (*Artemisia absinthium*) repels a number of pests, but don't sprinkle wormwood near brassicas as it inhibits their growth.

Spiders, slow worms

SPIDERS

Spiders have many strategies that make them highly effective pest-catchers. You often see spider webs constructed over inverted flowerpots. As insects emerge from eggs and pupae in the soil, they fly towards the light and are immediately caught by the spider as they come through the hole in the flowerpot.

Unfortunately, many people don't particularly like spiders, but they are fierce predators, constantly on the lookout for food. There are hundreds of spiders in every garden, and dozens of different species, but they are all gardeners' friends, as they attack many pests including most flies, spider mites, aphids, and moths.

SLOW WORMS

Snakes are rare in British gardens, and the easily identified adder, with a V-shaped mark on its head, is the only poisonous snake in the British Isles. Much more common are slow worms: shiny metallic brown snake-like creatures with a marked stripe on their back and darker brown sides. Shy creatures, they live in dark, quiet places such as under large stones, or in drystone walls. They are very good friends to any gardener as their main diet is slugs.

Planting to repel pests

When plants grow in the right conditions, in fertile soil, pest problems will be minimised. One way of ensuring the right conditions is to plant certain combinations that help each other.

Plant companionship works on many levels: plants can support each other by adding fertility to the soil, by offering protection from weather, from weeds, and from pests and diseases. Plants keep pests away from others by producing repellent chemicals, exuding a smell that puts plant-specific pests off the scent, and by attracting pests and trapping them.

Specific plants also provide a perfect breeding ground or food for helpful insects, so even when you are keeping the pest population down by planting repellent plants, you must also plant flowers to attract pest predators to control the pests that will break through your defences.

HOMEGROWN WARFARE

Marigolds (*Tagetes* spp.) are often quoted as miraculous companion plants, keeping pests, diseases, and weeds out of your garden. They do have an important role to play in pest control, as long as they are included as part of good garden practice. Marigolds produce a root exudation, or secretion, that discourages soil nematodes – tiny eelworms that attack and infest the roots of many plants. If you have a nematode problem in a vegetable bed, try planting a solid block of marigolds for a whole season and turning it into the soil like a green manure.

Members of the Allium family – garlic, onions, leeks, chives – seem to repel pests and prevent diseases. There's more research to be done, but one reason this seems to work is because Alliums donate excess minerals, including sulphur, to the soil, and excrete enzymes from their roots that seem to be toxic to many pests.

HELPING HANDS

If you are turning old pasture land into a productive garden, grow mustard before planting vegetables. Grassland usually harbours wireworms, the larvae of the click beetle. They feed on grass roots, so when you clear the grass they will feed on whatever comes next, particularly potatoes and other root crops. Luckily mustard is a favourite food and when you turn it under the soil in spring the larvae feed on it so greedily that they become beetles in record time and fly away to lay eggs in grassland elsewhere.

SCENT DETERRENTS

The strong scent of Alliums also repels insects that hunt by smell, as does the smell of the flowers and foliage of marigolds - particularly deterring whitefly and fleabeetle.

Most insects hate the strong bitter smell of rue (*Ruta graveolens*). It is particularly effective at keeping aphids away, and will even play a part in keeping four-legged pests off your garden if you plant it near entrances or around borders. Other strongly scented plants seem to confuse rather than repel insects that hunt by smell, which is why it's a good idea to plant strongly scented herbs near your brassicas or carrots to keep fleabeetles and carrot flies away.

Mint (*Mentha* spp.) repels many insect pests, including the cabbage butterfly – plant mint and the equally effective tansy (*Tanacetum officinalis*) in containers rather than in a vegetable bed as

Catnip (Nepeta cataria) smells too strong for many insect pests.

*If **lemon basil** (Ocimum citriodora) is planted in the garden close to tomatoes, it not only improves the taste of the tomatoes but deters white flies as well.*

Yellow *flowers attract insects to vegetable beds, where they can be caught in the flowers or on sticky traps and destroyed.*

The shoofly plant
(Nicandraphysaloides) is useful around greenhouses to attract and kill whiteflies.

Broad beans attract red spider mites.

Powdered rue (*Ruta graveolens*) is an effective cat, dog, and insect repellant, but it also seems to deter beneficial insects, it harms basil and slows the growth of tomatoes.

Tobacco plants (*Nicotiana alata*) attract whitefly.

Hoverflies and bees are apparently most attracted to blue/pink/red plants, while many pest insects go for yellow. Butterflies are attracted by pheromones, not colour.

Early-flowering plants such as wallflowers (Erysimum cheiri) and pot marigolds (Calendula officinalis) help beneficials get established early in your garden.

Favourite hoverfly flowers:

Buckwheat (*Fagopyron esculentum*)
Candytuft (*Iberis spp.*)
Cornflower/knapweed (*Centaurea spp*).
Dill (*Anethum graveolens*)
Morning glory (*Convolvulus tricolor*)
Mints (*Mentha spp*).
Phacelia (*Phacelia tanacetifoha*)
Poached eggplant (*Limnanthes douglasii*)

they are too invasive for open ground. Any herbs that give off strongly scented oils, such as lavender (*Lavandula* spp.), sage (*Salvia officinalis*) and rosemary (*Rosmarinus officinalis*) will deter many pest insects, while attracting some beneficial ones. Wormwood (*Artemisia absinthium*) is also excellent.

SACRIFICIAL PLANTS

Just as beneficial insects are attracted to specific plants, some plants are irresistible to pests. You can use this knowledge to trap insects on sacrificial plants, keeping your crops clean. Aphids, for example, can't keep away from nasturtiums, so they make good companions for apple trees and beans. The weed sowthistle (*Sonchus oleraceus*) lures leafminers as well as the lettuce root aphid. Pull it up in early summer and you'll remove numerous pests with it. You'll need to clear a patch of ground that has been infested with sowthistle thoroughly or pests and diseases will overwinter in remaining roots.

Planting to attract friends

Any pollen – and nectar-rich plants, such as yarrow and clover – will attract useful pollinators as well as predators. So it is important to mix and match your planting, maintaining a wide variety of plants that flower and fruit at different times. Even if your garden is largely down to productive crops, you should include some flowers, or let some crops flower. Predator wasps, for example, are particularly drawn to the flowering heads of parsley (*Petroselinum crispum*), and to flowering dill (*Anethum graveolens*) and fennel (*Foeniculum vulgare*), which also attract hoverflies and other beneficial insects.

Keep a patch of nettles (*Urtica dioica*) somewhere on the edge of your vegetable patch. Nettles are the breeding ground for the earliest hatching aphids, nettle aphids, which provide spring food for ladybirds coming out of hibernation. This means that your aphid-predator population gets going fast. To extend it at the other end of the season, ladybirds also love goldenrod (*Solidago officinalis*) and morning glory (*Convolvulus tricolor*).

Hoverflies and members of the bee and wasp family are attracted to many flowers, so diversity is the key, but try and find space for buckwheat (*Fagopyrum esculentum*) and phacelia (*Phacelia tanacetifolia*). As green manures, both these plants also have useful weed-suppressing and fertility-enhancing qualities.

Herbal lures

Strongly scented herbs attract many beneficial insects as well as deterring pests. Borage (*Borago officinalis*) attracts bees and predator wasps, and it also repels several harmful beetles. Hyssop (*Hyssopus officinalis*) attracts bees, hoverflies, and lacewings and seems to repel cabbage butterflies. Lavenders (*Lavandula* spp.) and mints (*Mentha* spp.) are also favourite plants for helpful insects; Tansy (*Tanacetum vulgare*) attracts ladybirds while discouraging ants and many soil pests.

Physical controls

Planting and good gardening practices are the first lines of defence against pests, but this may not solve all your pest problems, and you may also need to get physical. There are ways of making it difficult for pests to get to their favourite plants, and ways of despatching them when they do appear. You need to be vigilant and put physical controls into place before any pest problem gets out of hand.

Catching pests early is half the battle, so watch out for the first signs of pest damage and see if you can identify the problem by finding the pest or recognising the symptoms (see page 150). If you suspect a pest, check plants at different times of the day and evening as many pests come out at night.

Handpicking

Your hands are the most effective controllers for slow-moving pests. Whenever you see a pest insect just pick it up and squash it between your forefinger and thumb.

Handpicking works best on slow-moving insects, and on eggs and larvae. You can often find masses of eggs or caterpillars on the undersides of leaves, and larvae of many soil pests are often not far below the surface. Increase your chances of finding pests by creating special habitats for them – lay down some boards or piles of rotting vegetation for slugs to crawl under, earwigs will crawl into tubes or under rotting logs – then harvest them each morning.

If pests are too big to squash, drown them in a bucket of water with some vegetable soap added. You can compost them later.

Handpicking is best in early morning and evening, when it is coolest and dampest, or mount torchlight patrols to pick slugs off your plants when they are most active.

Handpick pests off plants in the early morning or evening when coolest.

Slug traps
Many creatures beside slugs like beer, including hoverflies, beetles, bees, and hedgehogs.

Traps must include a twig, so helpful creatures can crawl out, and some sort of cover to keep hedgehogs off the brew.

Sound advice
Badgers, foxes, and deer apparently keep clear if they can hear human voices at night, so you could try leaving a radio on.

Protect carrots from carrot fly with horticultural fleece.

Protect strawberries from bird damage with light netting.

Sticky traps

Make hanging traps by covering squares of card with something that stays sticky, such as tree grease. If traps are to be placed on the ground next to plants, or around their stems or trunks, purchase special vegetable or horticultural grease from garden centres or mail order catalogues. Sticky tapes are also available.

BARRIERS

The next best method is to erect barriers to stop pests in their tracks. These need to be put in place before a pest becomes a problem – it's too late when a pest has already colonised your crop. Sticky bands or tree grease around trees will prevent climbing insects, such as gypsy moth larvae, from climbing treetrunks, and prevent ant damage. Wrap and tie a heavy sticky paper band around the tree about 30 centimetres off the ground. Keep the sticky side off the bark.

Gritty barriers make life difficult for slimy-bodied slugs and snails, and fences may be the only way to keep four-footed pests out. You need to dig a fence firmly into the ground, burying 30–45 centimetres to deter burrowing creatures.

If you have serious rabbit problems you can buy electric fencing, but it is expensive and grass must be kept short around it or the fence will be constantly shorting out.

Horticultural fleece and lightweight covering fabric let in air, rainwater and light but are impenetrable by small insect pests such as fleabeetles.

Collars of card, foil, or carpet underlay around seedlings keep many soil pests at bay. Chopped-off plastic bottles protect vulnerable seedlings from most pests. Carrotflies never seem to fly higher than 60 centimetres, so a slightly taller barrier of very fine netting or polythene offers reliable protection.

Some fruit trees – particularly cherries – and soft fruit bushes will need to be netted if you want to get your fruit before the birds. If you don't net whole trees, cover bunches of grapes, or individual peaches and apricots with nets or brown paper bags as they ripen.

TRAPS AND BAIT

If you wear a yellow shirt on a sultry day before thunder you'll know just how many small flying insects are attracted to yellow. Sticky squares of yellow card hung above rows of vegetables may be all you need to keep many aphids, whiteflies, and fleabeetles off your vegetables. Yellow trap plants will attract them into a vegetable patch – then you can remove the plant plus its pests.

Pheromone traps (see page 149) emit chemicals that attract males of particular species to the traps with the lure of sex. They are most useful to monitor the population of orchard pests, such as codling moths.

Food and drink traps are part of the pest controller's armoury. Like many creatures, slugs find alcohol highly attractive, so pots of beer sunk into the ground, with the rims slightly above ground level, entice them to drink, and they drown. Where wasps become a nuisance you can trap them in jam jars filled with sugary water. Or trap pests by providing a meal of their favourite food, then picking and crushing or drowning them. Wireworms, for example, can be trapped by baits of potatoes or carrots.

You can also trap pests by providing refuges for them – earwigs will happily crawl into a cardboard tube in daytime, from where they can be gathered and disposed of.

SCARING PESTS AWAY

Bird-scarers, including scarecrows and mirrors in trees, have their place, and there's a theory that some animal pests will be frightened away if you mark your garden with the scent of their predators. Human hair in their path is said to deter rabbits and moles, and lion dung may keep cats and deer out. Cats will apparently flee from an inner tube masquerading as a snake! Don't rely on these, but they may help as part of a wider strategy.

Botanical pesticides

Some plants make effective pest controllers when they're harvested, but just because an insecticide is derived from a plant, this doesn't mean it is safe for humans and other mammals – strychnine is plant-derived, but you wouldn't want to get too close to that. The botanical insecticide nicotine, for example (from *Nicotiana tabacum*), works on insects' nervous systems so they convulse and die; humans can also be at risk if they are exposed to high doses of nicotine. Plant-derived poisons are considered safe in the garden because, regardless of how toxic they are, they break down into harmless compounds within hours or days when exposed to sunlight and they are easily decomposed by soil organisms.

PYRETHRUM, DERRIS, AND GARLIC

Pyrethrum, made from the dried and powdered flowers of the pyrethrum daisy (*Chrysanthemum cineranaefolium*), is one of the safest botanical insecticides as it harms specific pests and doesn't hurt mammals. Its active ingredient, pyrethrin, paralyses insects with

Organic pesticides should be used with restraint and as last resorts if you can't keep a problem under control by cultivation, through attracting beneficial creatures, or by physical measures.

Derris must be used very selectively as it can harm beneficials as well as pests.

an almost instant knock-down effect. Use pyrethrum against aphids, fleabeetles, and small caterpillars. Look for pure, powdered pyrethrum. Formulations that include piperonyl butoxide shouldn't be introduced to an organic garden.

Derris dust is made from the powdered roots of the Derris species. It kills insects on contact and acts as a stomach poison. However, although it harms a wider range of pests than pyrethrum, including aphids, thrips, red spider mite, fleabeetles, and sawfly larvae, it can also harm beneficial insects and it is poisonous to fish, so don't use it near ponds or streams.

An old folk remedy says that garlic can be planted to keep insects away from plants. Garlic contains allicin and other ingredients known to have insecticidal properties. Some people say garlic is effective against aphids and cabbage caterpillars as well as several pest nematodes.

Horticultural oils and soap spray

Horticultural oils have been used for centuries as a way to control pests on ornamentals and fruit trees – mineral oils were recorded by Pliny in the first century. They suffocate insects at all stages of growth by blocking their breathing holes, or penetrating the shells of insect eggs and interfering with the processes of maturation.

Modern horticultural oils can also be used on vegetable crops. Since oils act physically, they are safer to use than powders and sprays that affect pests' biochemistry. However, they are a relatively short-term measure. They can harm beneficial insects at certain stages of their growth cycle, and have to be reapplied regularly to get to grips with a large problem. Also, they can clog the pores and damage the leaves of any plants that are thirsty and needing to take in water when you spray. So only use oils at the coolest time of day.

SOAP AND WATER

Insecticidal soap spray is a safe way of despatching soft-bodied insect pests, including aphids, leafhoppers, mites, scale insects, and mealybugs. Insecticidal soap is a vegetable-based soap containing a mixture of potassium salts. The fatty acids in the soap penetrate the covering of soft-bodied insects and damage their cell membranes.

Susceptible insects become paralysed on contact so you need to spray the pest insects directly. Other insects become paralysed for a

Even the safest sprays can harm some creatures and plants.

Identify the problem and see if there is an alternative to spraying.

Only ever spray the infested parts, so don't blanket spray.

Soap spray must hit the pests directly to be effective, so it is best to spray when adults are not so active in the cool early morning.

To avoid drift, never spray in windy weather: only in still weather, so spray doesn't drift.

Never spray where bees are working. If there are hives in your area only spray in the evenings, when bees have finished for the day.

Don't use washing-up liquid in place of insecticidal soap. It's not designed for pest control and it can damage plants.

short time then recover. Slow-moving insects are more susceptible than those that can fly away from the spray, so soap sprays don't harm adult beneficial insects.

Soaps are a good emergency measure when there is a large and obvious build-up of insects on specific plants. They are virtually nontoxic to the user (unless you ingest a large quantity), they biodegrade into the soil very fast, and you can spray with them right up until harvest with no ill effects or lasting residues on the plants.

Biological controls

Sometimes a pest problem gets out of control, particularly if a garden has been neglected for a period, or rotation hasn't been practised so there's a build-up of a specific pest. Then you may also consider importing bacteria and pathogens that prey on pests – as well as encouraging their natural insect predators. Trapping insects by luring them with pheromones is another form of biological control. These methods of control are very effective against their target pests, but are highly selective, so pose no threat to the beneficial creatures or other organisms that you need to conserve in your garden.

MICROBIAL WARFARE

Microbial pesticides contain living micro-organisms that kill their host pests. They are purchased as powder, sprays, and granules to be reconstituted in water, then, applied as liquids or sprays.

The most widely used microbial pesticide is *Bacillus thuringiensis*, Bt. This is a bacterial species that only works on butterfly and moth caterpillars, and is inert until an insect eats it. Then it dissolves in the gut of susceptible insects, destroying the insects' digestive system and making holes in the gut wall. Bt is a useful control against the cabbage butterfly caterpillar, and some other caterpillar pests. The narrow range and specific activity of Bt means that no beneficial insects are killed by it and you can use it with other natural controls.

Another option is to introduce nematodes into your soil. These are tiny roundworms that prey on soil and aquatic insects and grubs, entering the bodies of their hosts and killing them by infecting them with bacteria that poison their blood. Nematodes can be effective in controlling slugs.

The main disadvantages of applying microbial controls are that they are very environmental-specific – as well as pest-specific – and need a controlled environment if they are going to be successful. If

Conservation of pest predators is the most easily available biological control. But it is just one option. Sometimes it is necessary to import biological controls as well as conserving those that already exist in your garden.

the temperature or conditions of the soil fluctuate much, the bacteria will be killed of – nematodes, for example, are particularly effective in a tunnel where conditions remain relatively constant. As microbial controls only act on pests at one specific stage of their development, you need to be vigilant to apply them at the best time – once susceptible caterpillars hatch into adults Bt has no effect.

As microbials are living organisms, they have quite a short shelf-life compared to botanicals or other controls. They are best used as part of a wider strategy, and only use Bt when you have a real problem as over-use may lead to pests ultimately adapting and becoming resistant to the bacteria.

Pheromones

Pheromone controls were developed for large-scale agriculture, but they can be very useful for any size of orchard. Pheromones are chemicals secreted and released by a particular species that elicit responses in other members of the same species. Sex pheromones are released to attract a mate, and you can purchase pheromone traps to control a variety of pests, including gypsy moths and codling moths. Unsuspecting adult males are lured into a sticky cardboard trap baited with female pheromones, or into a container with no exit.

Sex pheromone traps alone won't necessarily control a pest population as they only attract males, so they are most useful to monitor a pest population in order to select the best way of dealing with it. They highlight pest populations rather than destroying them. A possible disadvantage is that they may attract more pests into your garden, so never hang the traps near the pests' preferred habitats, but attach them to trees around the perimeter of the garden that the pests are not normally attracted to.

Genetic engineering of microbial pesticides

Microbial insecticides are targets for research in the biotechnology industry, where researchers are increasingly focusing on genetically enhancing the toxicity of microbes rather than looking at the possibilities offered by naturally occurring micro-organisms. The aim of much of the research is to increase the speed at which microbials kill pests, to make them less environment-specific, and to develop plants resistant to pests – such as genetically engineered pest-resistant tobacco and tomato plants. This may ultimately lead to the development of insect resistance to microbes, and a situation where Bt is no longer a useful insecticide.

How do I recognise and control common pests?

Recognising the problems

There are hundreds of species of insects in every garden. Most of them will never cause you much of a problem, so the following pages refer only to the commonest pests that you are most likely to come across, beginning with slugs and snails because these cause more obvious damage in more gardens than any other pest.

Earwigs and ants are sometimes thought of as pests, but they cause little damage and can be helpful as well as destructive. If they do cause you problems trap earwigs (page 146) and dispose of them, and disturb an ants' nest by digging through it and dispersing the colony. You can prevent them from climbing plants with sticky bands and barriers.

FRUIT PESTS

Soft fruit and tree fruit suffer from a variety of pests not found elsewhere in the garden. Codling moths are a major pest of apple and pear orchards; the caterpillars tunnel to the core of the fruits, but there's no evidence until the fruit is harvested. To protect trees, keep sticky grease bands in place to prevent the larvae climbing the trunks, and hang pheromone traps to catch male moths. Encourage bluetits by hanging fat in trees in winter, as they are major predators and can eat 95 per cent of codling moth cocoons over the winter.

BIOLOGICAL CONTROL IN THE GREENHOUSE

Red spider mites and whiteflies are two troublesome greenhouse pests. Spider mites are minute creatures found on the undersides of leaves. A severe infestation can kill a plant. Prevent the pests with good hygiene and maintenance, but if necessary you should purchase and introduce predatory mites (*Phytoseliuspersimilis*). Whitefly in the greenhouse can be controlled in the same way as other aphids (see page 153) or introduce the predatory wasps (*Encarsiaformosa*).

Some pests appear in nearly every garden. Learn about their life-cycles – how they breed, how fast they mature, and where they live in certain stages of development – so that you can decide on the best methods of control. Then pest control becomes common sense.

Fruit pests

Midges, mites, sawflies and other bugs can usually be controlled through good practice:

In autumn, lightly cultivate the ground round trees and bushes to expose larvae and cocoons; remove mulches so there are fewer places for pests to overwinter; and remove and compost any damaged fruit immediately.

If you do see pests, handpick them or spray with soap and water.

Slugs and snails

Slugs and snails are land-dwelling molluscs that move on one muscular foot on mucus slime trails. Most British gardeners wage a constant war against these greedy pests as they eat virtually any plant matter and can remain active almost all year where summers are damp and cool and winters warmish and wet. There is no instant way to solve a slug problem, but try a combination of methods and you should beat the pests.

Cultivation: Slug eggs are just about everywhere in the soil, but they don't hatch unless the conditions are just right. Cultivate soil well in spring to bring them up to the surface, where they can dry out and die.

Give young plants the best chance by transplanting seedlings from modules rather than sowing straight into the ground. When you mulch, keep it pulled back away from the base of your plants. If you lay black polythene for weed control, watch out! It acts like a luxurious slug hotel, warming up the soil and keeping it moist. So don't grow young plants or vegetables anywhere near that area.

Put decaying plant matter straight onto the compost. Don't leave it lying around. Keep your compost well away from vegetables. Slugs enjoy the warm, moist compost, and help break it down.

Handpicking: Slugs hunt most hungrily in the moist evenings so mount torchlight patrols to hand pick all the slugs you find. When they're not feeding they like a warm, dark atmosphere, so pay attention to the shady areas of your garden, and look under stones and piles of rotting vegetation, where they like to congregate. Turn stones over regularly and scrape off slugs and snails and their eggs. Drown them in water and feed them to ducks, or compost them. You need to handpick regularly to make a serious impact, but it is a useful control when seedlings are most vulnerable.

Slug pellets
Don't be tempted to use slug pellets for a quick fix. They may not solve the problem and they may harm creatures other than their target pests. The main ingredient in most slug pellets for gardens is metaldehyde, which dehydrates slugs. However, if it rains while the slug is dehydrating – which can take a day – the pest rehydrates. Metaldehyde works best in hot, drier conditions, which is when slug activity is lowest. Slug pellets get washed away in rain, they degrade in sunlight, and they only ever catch a small proportion of slugs.

Some pellets are based on methiocarb, which acts as a stomach poison.

Only about 4 per cent of a slug pellet is metaldehyde or methiocarb, the rest is a bait of ground cereal similar to dog food, which can attract other creatures. If something else snacks on pellets or a freshly poisoned slug, it may also be poisoned.

Predators: Encourage birds – thrushes and blackbirds particularly love snails. Encourage frogs, hedgehogs, toads, and slow worms. Ground beetles eat the pests and eggs. If you have space in

your garden, keep a few ducks and chickens.

Traps: Slugs love beer, and sinking shallow cartons or bowls full of beer at strategic points in your garden should encourage slugs to head for the traps rather than the plants. Only use beer traps until early summer or you risk drowning bees, too. Keep a stick in traps so that ground beetles can escape.

Try leaving eaten grapefuit halves, peel side up, among your plants, and slugs will gather underneath ready for disposal, or leave small piles of chopped-up juicy lettuce or comfrey leaves to provide pre-planned meals. Place these as far away as possible from the crops you are trying to protect, or you'll find the pests just move on to your other plants for pudding.

Barriers: Spread gritty protective barriers on the soil surface. These will need to be reapplied virtually each time it rains. Slugs and snails won't cross copper or they get small electric shocks, and don't like aluminium foil, so copper wire, copper-backed tape or foil collars round your favourite plants could help.

Biological control: You can buy nematodes that destroy slugs – put these microscopic parasites into the soil. *Phasmarhabdites hermaphrodita* enter the body of a slug and multiply inside them so that their host swells to a size where it no longer feeds, then burrows deep into the ground and dies.

Covers: To protect individual young plants and seedlings, make some fine wire mesh covers and place them over the plants. Glass or plastic cloches are also helpful and you can also use the tops of cut-off plastic bottles, but you have to be careful to move them when it's hot or you may roast your plants.

Slug barriers

Ash: Wood ash not only keeps slugs off but is an excellent feed for tomatoes. But avoid solid fuel ash and soot as they can contain small amounts of toxins that can alter the soil balance.

Bran: A tempting snack, which forms an absorbent and deathly barrier.

Grit (not for sandy soils): Fine grit also makes an attractive anti-pest mulch for plants in containers.

Sawdust (not for clay soils, where it can cause nitrogen starvation): Use sawdust from wood untreated with chemical preservatives.

Copper or foil barriers: copper tapes are now available that give slugs a small electric shock when they cross them.

Eggshells: Baking these shells before crushing makes them stronger, sharper, and longer-lasting.

Seafood shells: You can buy these shells from garden centres or pound your own. They are very decorative as well as repellent around ornamental plants.

Aphids

Some aphids are plant-specific; others move from one plant to another, and they can easily spread viruses if their mouthparts get contaminated. Some plants don't get much affected by the aphids; others produce twisted, curled, or swollen leaves or stems. Occasionally, aphids may actually kill leaves. They excrete masses of honeydew when they feed, which turns into black, sooty mould on leaves and stems, and attracts ants, flies and wasps, which can then become a nuisance. Although plants look rough when covered with sooty moulds, these don't damage the plant tissues. Once the aphids disappear, the sooty mould often dries up and falls off the plant.

Aphids are tremendous reproducers. The females give birth to tiny female nymphs that start sucking sap immediately, and the cycle of their birth to adulthood and producing new aphids only takes 10–14 days. So they tend to constantly re-infest plants. Some aphids have very complex life histories, living on several different host plants and overwintering on different species.

Aphids are sap-sucking insects found on many varieties of plant. They are widespread, but not hard to control. Blackfly start on the tips of plants – favouring broad beans, nasturtiums, thistles, and their relatives – then spread downwards. A severe infestation can spoil a crop of beans. Greenfly are most troublesome on ornamentals, especially roses, where they can damage the buds. Mealy aphids look as though they have been dusted with grey flour. They infest brassicas and cause distorted and discoloured leaves. Woolly aphids protect themselves by producing a downy coating. They commonly infest apple trees, attracting ants and wasps

and often harbouring disease. Lettuce root aphids prevent lettuces from developing fully.

Aphid controls
Cultivation: make sure plants are given best conditions and don't use too much nitrogen as this produces sappy growth, which encourages aphids.
Predators: Encourage predators by planting attractant plants (page 143) – ladybirds, hoverflies, lacewings, predacious wasps, and earwigs prey on aphids.
Barriers: Using fleece or other covers can protect against aphids and the diseases they transmit.
Handpicking: Squash on sight.
Companion planting: Plant aphid-hosting nasturtiums with apple trees. Plant wallflowers in orchards for early supplies of nectar, so that predators such as lacewings and hoverflies can get going early.
Resistance: Grow resistant varieties of lettuces.
Spraying: Soap and water. Hose woolly aphis with jets of cold water.

Caterpillars, cutworms, eelworms

Caterpillars
The large white or cabbage caterpillar is familiar to everyone who grows brassicas or verbascums. The cabbage white butterfly lays eggs on the undersides of leaves in May and July. The resulting yellow and black caterpillars feed hungrily, often completely stripping leaves.

Cutworms
The larvae of a group of moths, fat brown cutworms are up to 30mm long. Suspect them if your seedlings are nipped off at, or near, the ground.

Cutworm larvae start foraging in early spring. They eat at night, feeding on underground stems and roots and spend the day under surface litter near plant stems or in burrows in the top few inches of soil. Some species overwinter as eggs, others as larvae or adult moths. There can be four generations a year.

Eelworms
Eelworms are species of tiny transparent nematodes that attack tomatoes, potatoes, and cucumbers as well as some ornamentals.

Cabbage caterpillar control
Cultivation: Don't leave brassica stumps in the ground over winter. Grow brassicas with plenty of compost – this seems to help plants recover from any infestation.
Predators: Encourage predacious wasps – the ichneumon wasp lays its eggs in the bodies of the caterpillars.
Handpicking: Caterpillars are easy to find and pick off. Throw them into a bucket of water to drown them, then compost them.

Companion planting: Aromatic herbs seem to deter the butterflies, so plant sage, wormwood, lavender, and mint among your cabbages. Hyssop may attract the butterflies away from crop plants. **Biological controls**: Use Bt as your last resort.

CUTWORM CONTROL

Cultivation: Cutworms eat the roots of grasses and weeds as well as seedlings, so keep your ground clear of weeds, start seedlings in modules, and transplant them later.
Barriers: Surround young plants with collars of cardboard, newspaper, or even carpet underlay, to protect them until they are strong enough to withstand attack.
Handpicking: Clear the ground around seedlings in early morning and you can often find cutworms curled up into a C-shape. Rake them up and drown them. Gently scratch away the top 5cm of soil to find more in shallow burrows.
Predators: Ground beetles and birds feed on cutworms. They are hosts for some predacious wasps.

EELWORM CONTROL

Cultivation is the key to reducing eelworm. They are destroyed by mycelium-forming fungi, so soil that is well enriched with compost is a bad habitat for eelworms.
Companion planting: Root exudations of African marigolds (*Tagetes erecta*) kill pest nematodes.

Carrot fly & onion fly

Carrot fly (carrot root fly/rust fly)

The adult fly is smaller than 5mm, with a dark body, yellow legs and head, and red eyes. Flies lay eggs in late April and May on the soil surface around carrot plants. The eggs hatch in a week and the yellowish white maggots feed on and in carrot roots. After four to six weeks they change into brown pupae, which hatch in late July or August, when more adult flies emerge and lay eggs. This group causes plant damage into autumn. In a warm September more flies may develop to cause late damage. Carrot flies spend the winter as pupae in the soil or as maggots in the roots.

Onion flies

Resembling small houseflies, they emerge from the soil in May to lay their eggs on the soil surface near suitable plants. The emerging white maggots can be up to 1cm long, and they feed for three weeks on onion roots before pupating. Young plants can die, leaves of older plants wilt and the flies damage onion bulbs, which are then likely to rot. Like the carrot fly, there may be two or three generations a year.

CARROT FLY CONTROL

The maggots of this small fly can destroy your carrot crop, and may also attack parsnips, celery, and celeriac. Affected plants may become stunted, but usually the plant tops continue to look healthy. You know you've got problems if your carrots have dark patches and small rusty coloured tunnels through them.
Cultivation: You'll have least problems in light soil that is not over-manured. In some areas you can sow early to avoid the main egg-laying period; otherwise sow late, after the first flush of adults have emerged and dispersed. Wherever possible sow resistant varieties. Never leave carrots in the ground in autumn but lift them all in October so the pests can't overwinter.
Companions: Plant chives beside carrots to deter the flies.
Barriers: Cover rows of carrots with either horticultural fleece or fine mesh covers. Carrot flies don't fly higher than 60cm so erect barriers of polythene or fine mesh around the crops.

ONION FLY CONTROL

Onion fly pupae can remain dormant in the soil for many years, and can devastate an onion crop.
Cultivation: Try to sow onions before May, when there is the least chance of damage. Plant onion sets rather than sowing seeds as plants are most susceptible as young seedlings. Dig infected land in winter to disturb the overwintering populations of the fly. Make sure you practise rotation.
Barriers: Grow under a protective cover of fleece or cover.
Companion planting: Onion flies hunt by scent, so growing parsley and strong-scented herbs with or around onion crops can help.

Craneflies, fleabeetles, leafminers

Fleabeetles

These small, black, flying beetles can be a real nuisance in hot, dry summers. They arrive in clouds and can eat a row of young brassica seedlings overnight and make serious holes in leaves of larger plants. The first batch appears May to June, when temperatures reach around 20°C; the second batch August.

Leafminers

These greenish-white grubs, about 200mm long, infest many leafy vegetables, particularly spinach and beet. Flies lay eggs on leaf undersides. These hatch within four days and the larvae eat threadlike, winding tunnels within the leaves. As feeding continues the tunnels join together to make large light-coloured blotches filled with darker waste matter. Four generations are possible in a single season.

Craneflies

The larvae of craneflies/daddylonglegs can become a nuisance as they eat the roots of grass in lawns and can easily defoliate large patches.

Handpicking: Soak the lawn and cover it overnight with damp newspaper or carpet. In the morning lift the cover and grubs will have been brought to the surface. Drown and compost them.

Predators: Many birds feast on them, but they can also attract moles and even badgers into your garden.

FLEABEETLE CONTROL

Fleabeetles hunt in droves and can decimate a crop of young brassicas overnight by drilling the leaves full of tiny holes.

Cultivation and barriers: Careful timing of your sowing and planting can prevent the worst problems. Plant early if possible, under cloches or fleece, and cover germinating seedlings with fleece or lightweight row-covering fabric. Plant fast-growing brassicas again in July when the fleabeetles are dormant. Keep young plants well watered.

Traps: Hang yellow sticky traps above rows of brassicas to attract the beetles. If you run your hand over plants twice daily you'll catch large numbers as fleabeetles jump up when disturbed.

Botanicals: Use derris dust.

LEAFMINER CONTROL

Leafminers are the larvae of various small flies, beetles, and moths. They don't do too much harm, although they can check growth on young plants and make mature leaves very unsightly.

Cultivation: Dig in winter to destroy overwintering pests.

Barriers: Covers of horticultural fleece or row-covering material can prevent the insects getting a hold. Always pick off affected leaves.

Vine weevils

Vine weevil larvae are serious pests of a wide variety of plants. They are most often found in the compost of bought-in container-grown plants, but can also attack plants in open ground, particularly fuchsia, primulas, cyclamen, and begonias. Most houseplants are also at risk. Vine weevils devour the roots of their victims, but the first sign is not a creeping pest but usually a wilting plant that cannot be revived. Plants often keel right over or a gentle tug is all it takes to remove them from their compost or soil to reveal an absence of roots, and plump white grubs curled up in the container or 5cm below the soil surface.

Watch out: Whenever you introduce a new container plant, take it from its pot and check thoroughly for weevils and their larvae. If a plant, outdoors or indoors, wilts suddenly, check the root system without delay. If caught in time, plants can be saved through repotting or replanting. Never re-use infected compost unless you sterilise it well. Clean all pots thoroughly at the end of the season.

Cultivation: Dig ground in winter to bring grubs near to the surface, where conditions are too cold for them to survive, and birds can take them.

Handpicking: Adult vine weevils are relatively slow-moving and if you disturb them they usually lie on their backs and pretend to be dead so you can easily handpick them. All larvae should be dropped into hot water and destroyed.

Barriers: Put a strip of wide tape around individual pots and tubs, and smear this liberally with a non-drying glue, which the weevils cannot cross.

Biological control: You can buy nematodes that control vine weevils, but success depends on fairly constant temperature and soil conditions, and a plentiful supply of weevil larvae.

Adult vine weevils are matt black, about 1cm long, with a noticeable snout. They don't fly but climb to make holes and irregular notches in plant foliage. It is their larvae that are the real pests. These are up to 1cm long with a plump, creamy white body and a brown head. Female vine weevils emerge in early spring. Over a 3–4 month period they lay hundreds of eggs on the soil surface close to host plants. The larvae emerge after about two weeks, then tunnel into the soil, feeding on plant roots. As the weather cools in autumn larvae burrow to overwinter at a greater depth, and when it warms up in spring they pupate, and new adults crawl from the soil 3–4 weeks later.

In homes and heated glasshouses consistent warmth will enable weevils to be active all year round and to complete their life cycle more quickly.

Whiteflies & wireworms

Whiteflies

Often categorised with aphids, whiteflies have sucking mouthparts and feed on plant sap. They usually rest and feed on the undersides of leaves and fly off when disturbed. Affected plants have wilted leaves and are often coated with sooty moulds, but whiteflies rarely cause lasting damage.

Wireworms

These are a particular menace when you are gardening on recently converted old pasture land. Click beetles lay their eggs in summer and the larvae will feed in March to May and in September and October for up to five years before turning into beetles and flying elsewhere. They don't like to be disturbed so they feed quite deep in the soil, and one of the strategies for control is to provide lures to bring them nearer the surface.

CONTROLLING WHITEFLIES

Many species of whitefly – small flying insects about 2mm long – are common pests in the greenhouse, on houseplants, and on brassicas. The small white-winged insects live on the undersides of leaves, and plants can look as though they've been dusted with ash.

Cultivation: Good soil management and rotation will keep whiteflies at bay, and break the cycle of cabbage aphids by removing all plants in autumn.

Predators: Encourage the many aphid-predators with attractant plants.

Handpicking: Vacuum whiteflies off houseplants.

Spraying: Spray with soapy water or just use a hose – the water must hit the insects directly to have any effect.

CONTROLLING WIREWORMS

Wireworms are the slim orange-brown larvae of the click beetle, which can be up to 2.5cm long. They feed on roots and underground parts of grasses and vegetables. When you clear grass away they will feed on whatever comes next, particularly potatoes and other root crops.

Cultivation: When you clear old pasture land it is a good idea to grow a green manure crop of mustard (*Brassica nigra*) before planting vegetables. This encourages the wireworms to feed nearer the surface, and when you turn it under the soil in spring the larvae feed on it so greedily that they complete their life-cycle in record time and fly away to lay eggs in grassland elsewhere. Harvest crops by September to limit damage from autumn feeding.

Predators: Cultivation encourages wireworms near the surface, where birds can feed on them.

Traps: In small areas trap wireworms by punching holes in old food cans and filling them with bait of potato and carrot peelings or pieces of potato. Bury the cans so their tops are at ground level. Empty the traps every two weeks or so.

Birds, cats, & moles

Birds get wise to bird scarers, so you must change them regularly. It is reported that scarecrows are most effective if they are dressed in red!

Birds

Your garden needs birds to eat pests and aerate the soil, so welcome them, but keep them off your seedlings with barriers, or scare them off soft fruit and vulnerable crops. Cover young seedlings with chicken wire or cloches, and net fruit, or rig up webs of black thread. Birds get used to most scaring devices so you need to change them regularly, but half potatoes with feathers stuck into them seem to keep them off seedlings. Rows of hanging metal rods, old CDs, or flapping strips of plastic keep some birds away. Or you can buy commercial humming line to stretch above rows of vegetables – it glints and makes a noise in the wind.

Cats

Cats are a nuisance because they use your garden as a toilet. Find their toilet spots, clear away all the top layer of soil to remove the scent, and stick short, sharp twigs all over the area. You may have to do this several times to persuade the cats to go elsewhere. Reportedly you can keep them off your borders by draping a piece of hosepipe or inner tube in their favourite plants – apparently they think the tubes are snakes, and disappear fast.

Moles

Moles eat quantities of millipedes, cranefly larvae, and wireworms, but they also eat earthworms and they can do a lot of damage uprooting plants by burrowing under them.

They hunt by smell so you can send moles away by finding the end of a mole run, digging down until you see the tunnel and laying garlic, onions, or even old fish there before covering it up. Or try sticking partly buried empty bottles in the most recent molehills, or childrens' seaside windmills, and the sounds and vibrations may deter the moles. If this doesn't work, you may need to catch them in specially designed mole traps.

Mice, rabbits, badgers, foxes, & deer

All animals hunt by scent, so you can often keep them at bay by introducing or mimicking the scent of their predators. Badgers can be lured to another part of the garden with supplies of rotting fruit. It is illegal to shoot or trap badgers or wild deer – it is also illegal to pick up any animals that you run over on the road, but it's all right for the driver behind to take them.

Mice

Field mice can steal the seeds of early spring and autumn sowings of peas and beans, and eat many bulbs as well as nibbling root vegetables. Use physical barriers such as thorny twigs or cloches – or get a cat.

Rabbits

If young plants are chewed to the roots, and your vegetables disappear overnight, you've got rabbits. The only way to keep them out is with secure fencing, or you may have nothing left in your vegetable patch, and no young plants in your borders. Construct a sturdy wire mesh fence using maximum 5cm mesh. Dig a trench 30cm deep on the outside of the fence and firmly bury that depth of wire. If you can't fence, try tying clumps of human hair to sticks around your vegetables – rabbits don't like the smell.

Badgers, foxes, and deer

Once a badger has located your vegetable plot he will use it as his local deli and keep returning nightly, shifting almost anything you put in his way. Tying oil or creosote-soaked rags around the perimeter of your garden might deter them. Similarly, humming wires and jangling chimes can put them off. But if possible you should fence securely, nailing boards to the bottom of the fence and about 60cm up. Urban foxes also make a mess of your lawn and beds, digging for food and scent-marking. Very little seems to deter these modern day pests, who have moved into town to feed off our bountiful domestic waste.

Deer eat young trees and shrubs. Fencing them out of a garden is a mammoth task. Instead you need to protect all young trees with deer guards and preferably wooden and mesh cages – this also protects young plants from rabbits. Dumping lion dung around your garden perimeter is supposed to help, but the jury's out on this one.

The organic garden is a rich diversity of cultivated and uncultivated plants, wild and domestic animals – a productive mix of nature and nurture.

As with weeds, there is a place for tolerance when it comes to sharing your garden with wildlife. Not everything that moves in the garden needs to be exterminated. Even pests have a role to play in the wider web of interdependence that is our world.

Index

ACKNOWLEDGEMENTS

My thanks go to our designer, Bridget Morley,
for turning simple pencil sketches into
beautiful diagrams and keeping my overly
ambitious suggestions in check. Graham and
Nikki Elliot, Anne and Martin Wolf, and
Marion Gaze allowed us to wander over their
wonderful organic gardens at short notice
providing many appropriate subjects for
photography.

CINDY ENGEL

Photo credits
*All photography by Steven Teague except for
the following::* 39 Eric Crichton/**Corbis**, 87 left,
John Heseltine/**Corbis**, 87 right, Scott T.
Smith/**Corbis**; **Holt Studios**/ 84 Howard and
Linda Detrick, 90 Jean Hall, 97 U.Kroner, 41
top Nigel Cattlin, 41 bottom Primrose
Peacock; 2, 8, 14, 42, 44/45, 56 top, 60 top, 76-
81, 85-86, 93-94 left, 99-109, 110/111, 114, 115
bottom, 125-127, 131-132, Bridget Morley; 40
Seaspring Photos/Joy Michaud.
Photo-montages and artwork: Bridget Morley.